THE SECRET BIBLE
A SECULAR APPROACH TO THE BIBLE

Joseph R. Rosenbloom

Torah

Published in St. Louis, MO. by
Sts. Jude imPress.
Available for purchase on
www.jrrosenbloom.net, or
www.stjudesimpress.org
ISBN # 0-9766599-5-6
ISBN 10: 0-9766599-5-6
ISBN 13: 978-0-9766599-5-2

51990

9 780976 659952 $19.90

TABLE OF CONTENTS

SUFFIX

*Dr. Rosenbloom instructs – as is a
Professor's wont – concerning his
thesis and thrust of this book.* [1]

I TRUST MY READERS, WHO AS INTELLIGENT
INDIVIDUALS, ARE ABLE TO READ THE BIBLE
AND UNDERSTAND IT. THAT'S WHY THIS
BOOK DOES NOT CONTAIN THE
INTERPRETATIONS OF SCHOLARS AND OF
OTHERS WRITING ABOUT THE BIBLE FOR
ALMOST 2000 YEARS. FROM THE DAY IT WAS
CANONIZED, IT HAS BEEN ANALYZED.

MOST OF THOSE WHO HAVE WRITTEN ABOUT
THE BIBLE HAVE TRIED TO MAKE ITS
MESSAGE AS CLEAR AS POSSIBLE; THEY HAVE
INDICATED WHAT THEY CONSIDERED THE
PURPOSE OF THE TEXT. OTHERS HAVE
ATTEMPTED TO GUIDE THE THINKING OF
THEIR READERS IN ORDER TO HELP THEM
CONCLUDE THAT THEIR PARTICULAR
INTERPRETATIONS WERE WHAT THE ORIGINAL
AUTHORS HAD IN MIND. FOR THESE REASONS,
I PLACED NO FOOTNOTES IN THIS BOOK. THE
READER SHOULD BE THE FINAL ARBITER OF
WHAT THE BIBLICAL AUTHORS WERE TELLING
US.

WHILE IT IS CLEAR TO ME THAT THERE IS A
SECULAR BIBLE WITHIN THE BIBLE, THE
READER IS ADVISED TO KEEP A BIBLE AT
HAND TO VALIDATE (OR NOT) MY
CONTENTION, CONCLUSIONS AND
INTERPRETATIONS.

---

[1] *Editorial note: the synopses lying after each chapter # and its texts are the editor's not the author's. Any errors are the editor's.*

THE BIBLE, REFERENCE BOOKS, AND SCHOLARLY TREATMENTS OF EACH BOOK OF THE BIBLE THAT I SUGGEST FOR THE READER WILL BE FOUND IN MY BIBLIOGRAPHY AT THE END OF THIS BOOK. PUBLIC, SEMINARY, AND UNIVERSITY LIBRARIES WILL HAVE MANY OTHERS, INCLUDING THE SCHOLARLY JOURNALS, WHICH MAY DISAGREE WITH MY CONTENTION.

CHRONOLOGY OF ANCIENT ISRAEL

Pre-Monarchical (All Dates Are Approximate and are B.C./B.C.E. unless otherwise noted)

Abraham	~1800
Jacob's Family To Egypt	~1700
The Exodus –	~1250
Israelite Return To Canaan	~1200
Period Of Judges:	1200 – 1020
King Saul's Reign:	1020 – 1000
David:	1000 – 961
Solomon:	961 – 922

(Division Following Solommon's Death)

The Kingdom Of Judah [Judaea]   The Kingdom Of Israel
(Horizontal Lines Indicate A Change Of Dynasty)

KING	REIGN	PROPHETS	KING	REIGN
Rehoboam	922-915		Jeroboam I	922-900
Abijah (Abijam)	915-913			
Asa	913-873		Nadab	901-900
			Baasha	900-877
			Elah	877-876
			Zimri (7 days)	876
			Omri	876-869
Jehoshaphat	873-879	E L I J A H	Ahab	869-850
J(eh)oram	849-842		Ahaziah	850-849
Ahaziah	842	E L I S H A	J(eh)oram	849-842
Athaliah (usurper)	842-837		Jehu	842-815
J(eh)oash	837-800		Jehoahaz	815-801
Amaziah	800-783		J(eh)oash	801-786
Uzziah (Azariah)	783-742	ISAIAH HOSEA AMOS	Jeroboam II	786-746
			Zechariah (6 months)	746-746
			Shallum (1 month)	745

Jotham	742-735		Menahem	745-738
			Pekahiah	738-737
Jehoahaz	735-715		Pekah	737-732
(Ahaz)				
			Hoshea	732-724
			Fall of Samaria	722/I
			To Assyria	
Hezekiah	715-687			

M
I
C
A
H

Invasion of Judah by Sennacherib of
Assyria, 701

Manasseh	687-642
Amon	642-640

Josiah	640-609
Jehoahaz II	609
(Shallum)	
(3 months)	
Jehoiakim	609-598
(Eliakim)	
Johoiachin	598
(Jeconiah)	
(3 months)	

J
E
R
E
M
I
A
H

First phase of Babylonian Exile 598/597

Zedekiah	598-587
(Mattaniah)	
Fall of Jerusalem	587
to Babylonia	

Second (and major) phase of Babylonian Exile 587/586

Governor Gedaliah assassinated, 582

Third phase of Babylonian Exile 582

592-570	Ezekiel the Prophet in Babylonia
550-540	The Second Isaiah, prophet in Babylonia
539	First Return to Judah; Edict of Liberation by Cyrus of Persia
515	Zerubbabel and Josiah, secular and religious heads of Judea. Haggai and

Zechariah, prophets

in Judaea, Temple in Jerusalem rebuilt.

400   Second return to Judah, under Ezra. Jewish colonies in Egypt. Jewish theocracy established

in Judea by Ezra and Nehemiah. The high priests rule Judea.

300   Hellenistic civilization overwhelms Western Asia and Egypt, following on the conquests by Alexander the Great.

Chapter One

*It is proposed that the Hebrew
Bible - which originally was an
oral history of the Jewish people -
may have begun to be altered in the
eighth century BC and later added
to from royal court archives.*

PRELUDE

THE SECRET BIBLE: THE BIBLE WITHIN THE BIBLE is based on the thesis that much of the Hebrew Bible (HB) is essentially secular in nature: it deals with real-life situations and ideas in a way intended to enhance the lives of the Israelites. This is in contradistinction to its sacred overlay: God is the author of history and the controller of human events; thus, within this orientation, miracles abound.

The thesis is that from the eighth century BC/BCE on, Israelite society became more religious. The reason behind this was simple: to provide a means for the continuing survival of this people, whose more powerful neighbors repeatedly threatened, dominated, conquered and exiled them.

Secular accounts were joined with sacred stories to provide a specialty for the Israelites, and the motivation for their continued existence as a people. Editors completed this process perhaps as late as the third century BC/BCE [in this work, all dates are BC/BCE unless otherwise specified]. They produced the collection of documents, which have come to be known as the Hebrew Bible.

The complexity of the editing process has led to a plethora of scholarly speculation during the last two centuries: thousands of articles, monographs and books have put forth numerous analyses and theories:

"The Secret Bible: The Bible Within the Bible" is based exclusively on the text of the Hebrew Bible and focuses on the secular messages of the text.

The reader is encouraged to keep a copy of the Hebrew Bible available while reading this book. While various passages of the Hebrew Bible are cited, the reader may find more context helpful, and read verses before and after those reproduced.

To get even further into the texts, I suggest three other volumes for reference and background: The New Oxford Annotated Bible With the

Apocrypha, which contains an excellent translation with critical notes as well as helpful essays on the background of the text and introductions to each book; The Jewish Study Bible, published by the Oxford University Press, with another translation as well as essays on each book of the Hebrew Bible, supplemented by a wide range of traditional Jewish interpretations; and the HarperCollins Bible Commentary, which offers excellent essays on the historical background to Biblical society as well as summaries of each book of the Hebrew Bible with interpretations from much of contemporary scholarship. These books supplement the approach of this work and also serve as a balance to the approach followed in this book.

While the approach of this book runs counter to most analyses of the Hebrew Bible, it seems that the Hebrew Bible itself calls for an alternate orientation.

Chapter Two

*The author contends that the
original writers of the Hebrew
Bible were motivated for the
survival of the Jewish people and
their nation, not merely to promote
Monotheism.*

INTRODUCTION

Essentially, the Bible is a book of ideology, but not a unified ideology. The Hebrew Bible developed over a period of 2000 years. It thus has imbedded in it a variety of concepts, formed by many authors and traditions in response to the particular conditions of particular times.

In many of the books of the Hebrew Bible, one body of ideas may be blended with others: we find a classic example of this in the second chapter of the first book of Kings (I Kings 2.1-9). David, near death, offers advice to his son, Solomon, who is to be his successor. In the first four verses, he instructs him to obey God so that he and his successors will prosper. In its following five verses, he instructs Solomon to execute several people, including the general of the people's volunteer-army, Joab, and others against whom David had some grievance. The first verses follow the pattern of "sacred" history, while the latter are "secular," an instruction from father to son that is *real-politik*.

These ideologies had two basic purposes. One was to explain a given reality: why the monarchy was necessary, to motivate the people to obey a leader's commands by convincing them that retributive justice was reinforced by the laws given by God to Moses on Mt. Sinai.

The text of the Hebrew Bible is based on oral traditions. These were collected and recorded over time. Official court records were also a source, and were used primarily in the writing of the histories and poetry (Psalms) and the pronouncements of the Prophets. Biblical scholars tend to agree that the Pentateuch (also known as Torah, the Five Books of Moses) was completed in its present form in the fifth century. By literary and linguistic analysis, at least four separate traditions have been identified. They span perhaps six centuries from 1050 to 450; a number of viewpoints and philosophies have been incorporated into the text.

These traditions, or schools, were in 1878 first delineated by the German biblical scholar Julius Wellhausen. He identified four traditions, known as

J, E, D, and P. Scholarly work since has refined the details of Wellhausen's pioneering efforts.

- The earliest stratum, the J, or Yahwist, is so named for its preference of using YHWH for the divine name. It may have been first brought together by a contemporary of Solomon and represented the orientation of the south, the tribes of Judah and Benjamin. Where it can be isolated, it contains a more or less continuous story, from Creation until the entry into Canaan.

- The E, or Elohist, source favors using Elohim for the divine name. It is usually identified with the northern kingdom, the ten northern tribes that separated from the south after the death of Solomon and the ascension of his son, Reheboam, as king. It is probably later than J and more fragmentary.

- D, or the Deuteronomist, is comprised of at least two schools, and was written during the period of the destruction of the First Temple in 586. Central to its ideology was the centralization of worship and sacrifice in Jerusalem, and the concept of retributive justice. These authors' work is found in the Book of Deuteronomy and the histories, from Joshua through II Kings.

- P, or the Priestly school, was written after the Babylonian exile (after 586) and was primarily concerned with the Law to form a new basis for the community. Its vision for Israel was based on a religious hierarchy and emphasized the priesthood, the sacrificial cult, and the Temple, which could continue forever with or without a nation-state. Their focus was on the continuity of the people, after the destruction of the state and the exile.

It is assumed that sometime in the fifth century an editor or redactor combined the four traditions into the Pentateuch as it stands today.

There are many disagreements among those who study the Hebrew Bible, but most of them agree that the idea of God is at the center of almost every book. Secondary to God is the story of the Israelites and their relationship to God. The sacred nature of the Hebrew Bible is seen in the supernatural actions of the deity as he creates the universe and controls history: the creation of the cosmos, the punishment of the people for their sins by their being conquered and oppressed through the conquest and oppression of them by other nations, the giving of the Torah, the bringing down the walls of Jericho, the stopping the sun at Gibeon and the moon at Ayalon, and their miraculous victories over other peoples and nations.

Alongside this sacred quality of the Hebrew Bible is its secular aspect, in purpose and in literal form. By secular it is meant that events in the human realm are the result of human actions. For example, the books of Esther and the Song of Songs don't mention God. Much of David's history is also secular.

Thus, while some of the Hebrew Bible is clearly secular, other parts have secular elements embedded in them, such as secular court records reworked by religiously oriented historians. This was particularly true of the Deuteronomists, who put together the eight books from Deuteronomy through the second book of Kings, composed in the late Seventh to early Sixth Centuries (650-550). Similarly, the Priestly school of the Sixth and Fifth Centuries (600-400) reveals its imprint especially in the first four books of the Torah (Genesis, Exodus, Leviticus and Numbers), particularly those sections dealing with the priesthood, the Temple in Jerusalem, and the sacrificial cult.

Much of what appears to be sacred is sacred in form but essentially secular in motivation and purpose. This is particularly true of the various law codes found in the Torah. According to the Torah, God promulgated all of these laws. But the laws not related to the priesthood and cult are clearly secular. They developed, as is true of all law codes, to protect property and the rights of the powerful, and to bring order to the society.

Many of these laws were also a part of the general legal patterns of other societies in the area, particularly in Mesopotamia. Having God as the Source of the law served to reinforce its validity. Having God as the Enforcer served as motivation for the people to obey the law or suffer the consequences at the hands of God's appointed officials or through God's direct acts.

While ostensibly sacred, the overall purpose of the ideologies was in fact secular: the survival of the Israelites as they struggled to live through a succession of dramatic political and social changes during the biblical period, from 1200-450.

The first challenge came during the invasion of Canaan, when the Israelites were confronted by an advanced culture, which threatened to absorb them. The code word for defense against this threat was 'idolatry.' The reality of the time was that the Israelites were also idolatrous but the later Deuteronomic historians recast the religious nature of the people as having been monotheists back to the time of Abraham (1800). The Book of Judges portrays their constant backsliding as idolatry. It is clear, however, from the last chapters of the Second Book of Kings, that Judaean society, while ostensibly monolatrous, was thoroughly polytheistic. The challenge from Canaan and the nations in the immediate area was also met by the establishment of the monarchy first, and ineffectively by Saul, and then successfully by David.

The second great challenge came as a result of the conquests, first of the kingdom of Israel (the ten northern tribes) by Assyria in 722, and then of the kingdom of Judaea in 586. The exiled Israelites, with little identifying culture and religious ideology of their own, were readily absorbed into the population among whom they now lived. The memory of this perceived disaster led religiously oriented thinkers, writers and scribes to develop ideologies which served to explain the reality of the captives and to motivate them to survive as a special people. The leading ideologues were the Prophets, revealing and teaching, as they believed God had instructed them. The main prophets of survival were Jeremiah, Isaiah of the Exile and Ezekiel. While their rhetoric was sacred, their purpose was secular.

The Purpose of this book is to outline the essential secularity of the Hebrew Bible while acknowledging the pervasive sacredness of the structure of the text. There are three kinds of texts: the totally secular; those, which are secular but embedded within a sacred structure; and those, which are totally sacred.

The purpose of all of the authors of the Hebrew Bible was the survival of the Jewish people. The religionizing or sacralizing of the Bible seems to have begun with the prophet Amos in the mid-eighth century. He may have been the first to intuit that the national enterprise of Israel was doomed in the long run, and that the survival of the people demanded a new set of ideas and raison d'être for their existence.

It began with Amos but much was added over the next three centuries by such prophet-ideologues as Hosea, Michah, Jeremiah, and Isaiah of the Exile. They provided a sacred overlay to what had been an essentially secular society while embedding secular values in their writings. This is clearly seen in their devaluing of the Temple sacrificial cult, the major symbol of the sacralized society.

Chapter Three

*It is taught how Torah was edited
by a new generation of priests
educated during their 586
Babylonian Exile.*

PENTATEUCH:

THE TORAH; The FIVE BOOKS OF MOSES

The central documents of the Hebrew Bible are included in the Pentateuch, also known as the Torah and the Five Books of Moses; God's revelation to Moses on Mt. Sinai two years after the 'Children of Israel's' Exodus from Egypt. Such a revelation served to add tremendous authority – and make Torah binding on a future Israel. These books are a composite of ancient oral and written traditions going back centuries before editors finalized them - probably in the fifth century.

The edited text has the stamp of the leaders of a Judaean society coming into being after the return from exile; some seventy years after the 586 conquest of Judaea by Babylonia with their destruction of the Temple in Jerusalem. The community's leadership was the priests, placed in power by the Persian king: Israel had been transformed from a monarchy to a hierocracy where the priesthood dominated.

The rationale for the community was a sacralized one; it was tied to the one true God, led by the Aaronite priesthood and assisted by the Levites. The Pentateuch's final editors structured it to validate this approach, through the holy text as dictated to Moses by God.

As such, the Pentateuch reflects a sacred orientation. Still, secular narratives are interspersed in the text. While the purpose of these books is the survival of a people in their *specialness*, it was to be carried out by a thoroughly sacred approach.

Chapter Four

Genesis is presented as a secular history of family conflicts among the Patriarchs. It synopsizes Adam as child-like, Abraham as obedient, Isaac as passive, Jacob as a trickster, and Joseph as vengeful, when they otherwise are not exemplar Patriarchs.

GENESIS

The book of Genesis sets the stage for the rest of the Hebrew Bible: it covers the period from the creation of the universe up to the Exodus, when the Israelites were freed from slavery in Egypt.

Genesis' first eleven chapters describe primeval history, while the remaining thirty-nine deal with the founding fathers, the Patriarchs of Israel: Abraham, Isaac and Jacob. God is the central element in all of these narratives except for the Joseph cycle (37.1-50.26) as well as other minor exceptions (46.1-4). Central to Genesis are God's dealings with the world, and Israel's special role in God's purpose.

The priestly writers and the final editors, with God central to their belief system, used the first chapter of Genesis as the general introduction to the Hebrew Bible. In it, God is the creator of the universe and everything on Earth as well. This indicates the absolute power of the one, single, unique deity, far superior in every way to the multiplicity of gods of the other peoples of the region. God is not only the creator but is also, by implication here and explication elsewhere, in control of nature and history.

The above-mentioned writers clearly had a sacred approach to reality. It also served a secular end: it provided Israelites security from an all-powerful deity who is tied to them by a special covenant established with the first Hebrew, Abraham. And human beings, realizing their frailty before the forces of nature, received an additional sense of power and specialness in nature: they were created in the image of God who awarded them control over nature (1.1-2.4a).

In Genesis' next ten chapters, another central ideological issue appears: obedience to God is to be rewarded; disobedience is to be punished. God is seen to be in charge of history, a theme often repeated throughout the remainder of the Hebrew Bible.

ADAM

In the other creation story (Gen 2.4-3.24) God is viewed quite differently. Rather than being omnipotent, transcendent, and existing far above in space, he is viewed anthropomorphically: walking in the Garden of Eden; creating the first man, Adam, from earth; creating the first woman, Eve, from Adam's rib; while walking in the garden and seeking Adam and Eve, he doesn't know where they are (3.9).

These first humans are given Paradise, a perfect existence with just a single condition: they may eat anything in the garden except from the trees of knowledge of good and evil, and from the tree of life (2.9, 16-17; 3.22-24). Like children, they almost immediately do the one thing forbidden them. After they eat from the tree of knowledge, they are punished, and prevented from eating from the tree of life. Disobedience is to be punished: a theme repeated throughout the Hebrew Bible. In Paradise, humans seek to be like God, having knowledge and immortality.

While set in a sacred framework, it can be secularly translated as an innate human bias against authority: the power of God allows the faithful to do whatever one wishes but they face the consequences of their actions.

Biblical passages demand that they have freedom in order they may be held accountable for what they do. This theme is repeated in the story of the Tower of Babel when humans build a tower to heaven:

> " ... nothing they (humans) propose to do will now be impossible for them" (11.6). Secular elements in the Tower of Babel story include the origin of the multitude of human languages while ridiculing Israel's enemy Babylonia as an unnatural polyglot empire (11.6-9).

Following its Babylonian Exile, Israel had no king, and established society requires obedience to its king and its legal structure. As a result, the post-exilic priestly leaders used the power of God and their special role as his direct agents to maintain order. The flood story accomplishes the same goal: the people were thoroughly evil and were to be washed clean. Only Noah,

> "a righteous man, blameless in his generation," together with his family and animals, would be rescued to give humanity another opportunity to do the right thing (6.9; 6.1-9.17).

A rationale for conquering Canaan is found at the end of the Noah story. While Noah was sleeping off a drinking episode, his son Ham, the father of Canaan, viewed his father's nakedness. God would bless Shem, presumably standing for Israel, and Canaan would be his slave (9.20-27).

The Cain and Abel story appears to disallow capital punishment. Cain who killed his brother, Abel, is not to be killed but condemned as a fugitive and wanderer (4.8-15). Established society requires obedience to its legal structure. The story also affirms the superiority of farmer over shepherd. Although the shepherd is preferred (Abel's sacrifice is favored by God over Cain's), historical reality has the farmer as the more productive and more powerful; the farmer may also symbolize the idolatrous practices of the Canaanites among whom the Israelites lived influencing them in harmful ways (4.1-5).

While the existence of an all-powerful God and retributive justice are the major themes of the first eleven chapters of Genesis, several other essentially secular elements are interspersed; the punishment for eating from the forbidden fruit leads to Adam's having to earn a livelihood under difficult conditions; Eve not only to bear children in pain but also to be subservient to Adam (3.16-18); prevented from eating from the tree of life, they were denied immortality (3.19, 22-23) (while immortality is negated in the Torah, it is affirmed elsewhere in the Hebrew Bible, particularly in Isaiah, the Psalms and the Book of Daniel. In the post-biblical period, this issue would divide the Sadducees from the Pharisees and Essenes).

THE PATRIARCHS
ABRAHAM the Patriarch
Chapter 12 introduces the story of the Israelites, the great theme of the rest of the Hebrew Bible. The first Hebrew, Abram (later, Abraham; 17.5), is the father, the patriarch of the people who became known as Israelites, named for Abram's grandson, Jacob/Israel.

Its narratives establish Abraham as the exemplar of those who followed him. Just as the introductory chapters of Genesis establish the necessity of being obedient and faithful to God, so is Abraham the exemplar of obedience. When he was commanded by God to leave his homeland and family, he did so without hesitation. God assured him that: his progeny would evolve into a great nation; he would be a blessing to others; and be protected by God (12.1-4).

His faithfulness was reinforced by his willingness to sacrifice his son, Isaac, at God's command. Once God realized that Abraham was faithful and feared him, Isaac was spared, when a ram was substituted as a sacrifice (22.1-19). Abraham was the model for his people who should equally be entirely obedient to God.

That Abraham was not totally passive before God is indicated in the story of the wicked cities, Sodom and Gomorrah, which God planned to destroy. Abraham advised God that he had to meet the ethical standard of not killing the innocent with the wicked (18.22-33). The sacred lesson is clear: God is in control and humans are to obey him and follow the laws he ordained. Abraham's faithfulness is to be emulated so that his progeny will prosper. Spreading this ideology throughout Israelite society would help it to become stable.

ISAAC the Patriarch

Two experiences, which Jacob had with God, show the varying views found throughout the Hebrew Bible. They appear to contradict the orientation of Abraham offered in Genesis.

- Jacob cheats his twin, Esau, out of his father's blessing, and is sent away by his mother out of fear that Esau will take revenge on him. In another version, Isaac sends Jacob away so that he would not marry a Canaanite but someone of their family (27.41-28.5).
While Jacob slept on his way to his mother's brother, Laban, he had a dream. In this dream God renewed his promises to Abraham and Isaac that Jacob would be blessed with abundant offspring and the land earlier promised. Upon awakening, Jacob made a vow that " If God will be with me (providing food, clothing and protection)…then the Lord shall be my God." (28.10-22).

Here, Jacob's faith is conditional, in total contrast to the faith of Abraham.

- The second experience occurs during the evening before he was to meet Esau. Here, Jacob wrestles with a 'man' who is, in reality, God. Jacob is wounded, but he's still asked to release his opponent. God tells him,
"You shall no longer be called Jacob, but Israel, for you have striven with God and with humans, and have prevailed." (32.22-32) {Israel=one who strives with God}

Jacob/Israel again offers a direct contrast to Abraham. Faith is to be earned, even by God, and humans are allowed to struggle with God. In a secular sense, it means that the Jewish people are not to simply accept what God or his representatives' demand without discussion and dissent.

The remainder of Genesis deals with Abraham's progeny. While God is occasionally present in these narratives, they are essentially secular accounts of families interacting with one another and their neighbors. These interactions most often take form as argument and conflict.

It did not take long for conflict to occur among the Hebrews.

- Shortly after they returned from Egypt, Lot's herdsmen quarreled with those of Abram. Once again, Abram was a model, here of conciliation:

"Let there be no strife between my herdsmen and yours, for we are kinsmen" (13.8).

While Lot took a preferable territory, it was to his long-term hurt: he settled near Sodom whose inhabitants

"were very wicked sinners against the Lord" (13.13).

- A three-way conflict takes place between Sarah, Hagar and Abram. Because Sarah believed that God prevented her from bearing children so she told Abram to engage in sex with her Egyptian servant, Hagar, so that she (Sarah)

"might be 'sonned' (built up) through her" (Hagar) (14.2). Once she became pregnant, she held her mistress in low esteem (14.4). Amazingly, Sarah blames Abram: "The wrong done me is your fault!" (16.5).

Abram, ever a man of peace, said:

"Your maid is in your hands. Deal with her as you think right. Then Sarah treated her harshly, and she ran away from her" (16.6).

Through divine intervention, Sarah finally becomes pregnant although she is ninety and Abraham is one hundred: nothing is too difficult for God (21.1-7; 18.9-15). The friction between Abraham and Sarah continues after Isaac is born. Sarah tells Abraham to

'cast out this slave woman and her son, for the son of the slave shall not share in the inheritance with my son Isaac.' The matter distressed Abraham greatly, for it concerned his son." (21.10f.)

- The Patriarchs, Joseph and others in Genesis frequently had conflicts with women or because of women: Adam with Eve; Abraham with Sarah and Hagar; Isaac with Rebecca; Jacob with Rachel; Reuben with Bilhah; Judah with Tamar; Joseph with Potifar's wife. Symbolic of his situation with Sarah is the biblical account of her death. Half of a verse announces her death and another half tells of Abraham's mourning and wailing for her (23.3). Seventeen verses are devoted to his acquiring a burial place and burying her! (23.4-20). Isaac, Sarah's favorite, could only find comfort from his grief with a wife (24. 67).

No such language is used for Abraham.

"Abraham" simply "took another wife, whose name was Keturah" (25.1),

bearing him six sons; he apparently had many others by his concubines (25.2, 6). Could her long-time inability to produce children be the result of on-going incompatibility and conflict between them? While biblical tradition values women and there are some exemplary examples, conflict generally characterizes relations between the sexes.

No biblical personality was more engaged in conflict than Jacob. Before his birth until he was near death, conflict characterized his life. Directly or indirectly, he is involved in the remainder of Genesis. All Jews descended from Abraham and Isaac are "b'nei Yisrael," 'children of Israel.'

The twelve tribes, really thirteen (Jacob's twelve sons are supplemented by Joseph's two, Ephraim and Manasseh, to compensate for the non-territorial Levi from whom the priests are descended), comprise the Jewish people. All of the previously outlined issues and conflicts are replicated in the Jacob traditions. However, in each instance, the narrator introduces stories which are both the same and different, repeating lessons but enriching the messages while adding to them.

- Jacob's father, Isaac, is the weakest of the Patriarchs. Isaac is problematic, a victim of conflicts and the aspirations of those with whom he is involved. Passivity is his hallmark. He is even absent from his own betrothal scene; his servant, Eliezer, not he himself is sent to find a suitable wife from among his Mesopotamian kinsmen (24.2). If this woman is unwilling to return to Canaan, Isaac is not to be brought there nor is he to marry a Canaanite woman (24.3-9).

Presumably, Isaac would not marry, and Abraham would have no sons to succeed him. Family wealth would devolve to Eliezar, who, being from Damascus, was not a Hebrew (15.2f.). Substituting a servant for Isaac as possible heir and in the betrothal process fits with Isaac's entire Curriculum Vitae. He was a bound victim for whose life a ram was substituted; he will later prefer the son who can go out to the field and bring back venison; in his one extended scene, he is portrayed as lying in bed, weak and blind, while others act on him (23.1-46).

Contrasting father Isaac's passivity, his major foe, Rebecca his wife-to-be, is a continuous whirl of purposeful activity. The biblical narrator contrasts her with Isaac in four short verses in which she is the subject of eleven verbs and one speech, in the scene wherein she first meets Isaac (24.16, 18-20; recapitulated in 45-46). She also takes the initiative at a crucial moment in order to obtain the paternal blessing for her favored son, Jacob (27.1-17). Her power, rather than Isaac, is made clear when words usually associated with Patriarchs are conferred on her when she is blessed by members of her family as she is leaving them for Canaan:

"O sister! May you grow into thousands of myriads, may your
offspring seize the gates of their foes" (24.60).

As Jacob's mother set the stage by her dominant nature, so Jacob would, with his mother's connivance, carry on against both his father and brother.

- The conflict between Jacob and his twin brother was said to be determined by God before their birth:

"Two nations are in your womb, two separate peoples shall
issue from your body. One people shall be mightier than the
other and the older shall serve the younger" (25.23).

During the birth, Jacob tried to get out first, emerging holding on to Esau's heel (25.26). Because he was holding onto his brother's heel, he was called 'Jacob' [Yaakov] from the Hebrew for heel, 'akev.' Ya-a-kov is the future form of akav which might also mean 'he will overreach.' (We might read it as, 'he will (be a) heel.' This root is also used in the Bible to mean, circumvent, deceive or defraud).

The Biblical narrator deals only with what he considers essential.

- Following their birth, our first encounter with the twins finds Jacob, 'the mild man who dwells in tents,' 'cooking a stew,' while

Esau, 'a skillful hunter (was) a man of the field,' returned home 'famished' (25.27, 29f.). Esau requested some of the food because 'he was famished,' subsequently saying, "I am at the point of death." Jacob would feed him only in exchange for his birthright. A simple exchange was not sufficient for Jacob. He had Esau take an oath (25.30-33).

- "Isaac favored Esau because he had a taste for game, but Rebecca favored Jacob" (25.28). The family relationship is summarized in that homey statement.

- The next episode involving all four begins with Isaac - old, blind and soon to die - asking Esau to prepare his favorite food, which is to be followed by a special blessing. Rebecca, overhearing this conversation, connives with Jacob to get the blessing for himself. He was to fetch two choice kids and, while she is preparing them appropriately, he would disguise himself to deceive his father into believing he was Esau in order to gain his father's blessing. Rebecca puts aside his fear of discovery

"Your curse, my son, will be on me" (27.20).

God is now implicated in his deceit. Twice more, Isaac asks,

"are you my son Esau or not?" and "are you my son Esau?" (27.21,24).

Even after Isaac touched him, heard his "voice which is the voice of Jacob,

" kissed him and smelled him; he still blessed him (27.21-19).

Could Isaac have been as blind and unaware as he claimed? Was all of this God's plan so that he was helpless before destiny? First, it appears that he was truly unaware: when Esau returned and identified himself: "Isaac was seized with very violent trembling," (27.33) but, almost immediately stated, "Your brother came with guile and took your blessing" (27.35). The conflict between the brothers and their parents reaches its climax. As God had prophesied to Rebecca while she was pregnant, "the older will serve the younger." Now Isaac confirms to Esau:

"you shall serve your brother, but when you grow restive, you will break his yoke from your neck" (25.23; 27.40).

A secular explanation would resonate more effectively in human terms. The situation may be viewed as a family drama in which a submissive husband is hated by his domineering wife. The submissive father encouraged in Esau what his aggressive mother repressed: the freedom of a hunter. The mother favored homebody-Jacob, whom she could dominate as she could not the freer Esau.

Each twin was only half loved. Insufficiently loved by his passive father, Jacob was filled with fear. Insufficiently loved by his strong mother, Esau was filled with hate. It took the therapy of life's hardships before the twins matured sufficiently to respect one another and become reconciled. Even then, however, Esau had grown more; Jacob was still fearful (32.8; 33.1-15).

Rebecca realizes that the conflict is not completed: Esau plans to kill Jacob after his father's death. She is also fearful that he will marry a Hittite woman as Esau is said to have done (26.34f.). She, therefore, sends him to her brother's home to escape - and find a suitable wife (27.41-45; 28.1f.).

The passage regarding Esau's Hittite wife seems to be contrived. Her name is Y'hu-dit, Judith, Jewess. The purpose may be to rationalize the events of the next chapter. 28.6-9 would seem to indicate that Esau only took Canaanite wives after losing his father's blessing:

"Esau realized that Canaanite women displeased his father Isaac."

In these three narratives regarding Jacob, we find him in the first of a series of trials and tragedies, which will dominate his entire life. Human reality is portrayed through his labyrinthine life of conflicts, antagonisms, reversals, deceptions, shady deals, outright lies, disguises and misleading appearances. Holding onto anything concrete fully or for long is difficult for him. Just as Jacob duped his father, so is he over and over again to be deceived, proving himself to be blinder than his father by mistaking his first wife, Leah, for Rachel on their wedding night (29.21-25).

JACOB

Jacob's life in his new home with his uncle, Laban was to be as conflicted as had been his younger life among parents and brother. His first act in his new home is symbolic of his difficulties: removing a stone from the mouth of a well, one more obstacle to overcome (24.2f.). Soon he would, for seven years be blocked from marrying Rachel, while her most fertile years were passing. His whole life would be rocky. As he was a 'heel-grabber' or wrestler, a contender, the man who seizes his fate, tackles his adversaries, so does he seize the rock atop the well with his own two hands. He also sleeps on stones, speaks in stones, wrestles with stones, contending with the hard unyielding nature of things.

Jacob's first difficulty comes in a conflict with his future father-in-law.

- Promised Rachel after seven years of labor, Jacob, who had weak eyes like his father's is presented her older sister, Leah; he is deceived just like he had deceived his father. It is rather strange that Jacob did not discover the deception until the next morning after having sex with her (24.17, 23,25).

Unsurprisingly, the first pair of sisters encountered in the Hebrew Bible duplicate the first conflict between brothers Jacob and Esau. Rachel was envious because Leah had many sons; Leah was envious because Jacob loved Rachel more. As Sarah had been 'sonned' initially by her handmaiden, so was Rachel through Bilhah.

Rachel makes it clear that this was understood as a battle. After Bilhah bore Jacob a second son, Rachel declared:

"A fateful contest I waged with my sister: yes, and I have prevailed" (30.8).

When Leah stopped bearing, she continued the competition through her maid, Zilpah. Apparently, Jacob had stopped sleeping with Leah but she bought an evening with him for some mandrakes. They did not work for Rachel, but Leah succeeded and had two more sons and a daughter (24.30-30.21). We find here a replication of the whole series of struggles between older and younger brothers, with repeated drives by the younger to displace the firstborn.

- Jacob's on-going conflict with Laban culminates with his success in crossbreeding sheep and goats after his father-in-law attempted to short-change him. This time Jacob's skill wins out over Laban's unfairness (30.25-43).

Abraham loved Sarah, but their relationship was less than ideal. This same is true of Isaac and Rebecca. There was no real courtship (24.64-67), and their family was deeply conflicted. There is much more expression of love on the part of Jacob for Rachel and she for him, than with those others. It was love at first sight, and he worked fourteen years for the right to marry her.

Yet even the most ideal marriages have conflicts.

- Though Jacob openly professed his great love for her – greater than his love for Leah - her resentment was great because she could not have children. Finally, she blamed Jacob:
  "Give me children or I shall die" (30.1).

Jacob's response may have begun a gradually growing resentment toward her for all of her nagging.

"Jacob was incensed at Rachel and said, 'can I take the place of God, who has denied you fruit of the womb?'" (30.2).

After all, he had produced sons with Leah, and soon would with Bilhah and Zilpah as well.

There is no direct evidence of any conflict between Jacob and Rachel other than these two verses. However, Jacob's hostility may have been unconscious. In a sense, it was he who determined her premature death. As Jacob was preparing to return home, Rachel stole her father's teraphim, doubtlessly to keep their power from him and to aid them on their journey. When Laban searched for them in her tent, she lied to her father. Previously, when Laban asked Jacob why he stole his gods, Jacob answered:

"'anyone with whom you find your gods shall not remain alive!'...Jacob did not know that Rachel had stolen them" (31.19,32-34).

- During Rachel's next childbirth, she died (35.16-20). Could her premature-death be the result of her conflict, her disloyalty toward her father? What we may assume is that Jacob, by his rash oath, unwittingly brought on his beloved's destruction. Another possibility is that Jacob knew of her theft, at least unconsciously, and was striking out against her. Perhaps his anger toward her was greater than he could acknowledge. One earlier wife, his mother, had caused him abundant difficulty and he may have known something of the trouble Abraham had with Sarah. Ironically, the only instance when Jacob was overtly angry with Rachel was when she blamed him for her sonlessness (asking for sons not a son). The birth of a second son resulted in her death.

Another of Rachel's faults was her theology. Unlike Sarah and Hannah, she turned to the power of her husband rather than God. While her son Joseph would rise to great heights, the future kings of Israel would come not from him but from Judah, the fourth son of Leah.

Two episodes continue Jacob's conflicts with his children. Simeon and Levi slaughtered the inhabitants of Shechem for raping their sister, Dinah, after Shechem promised to marry her.

> "Jacob said to Simeon and Levi: 'You have brought trouble on me...my men are few in number, so that if (the Canaanites and Perrizites) unite against me, I and my house will be destroyed.' But they answered, 'Should our sister be treated like a whore?'" (34.30f.)

And:

> "...Reuben went and lay with Bilhah, his father's concubine and Israel found out" (35.22).

Before continuing with the Jacob narrative, which involves Joseph and his brothers, there is an interrupting interlude. It begins with another filial conflict.

- Judah married a Canaanite who bore him three sons; the wife of his firstborn, Er, married Tamar. When he died without children, Judah told his second son, Onan, to perform the duty of brother-in-law to provide offspring for his brother. He performed coitus interruptus repeatedly since he knew

"the seed would not count as his" (35.9)

He died and Jacob promised Tamar, his third son Shelah when he grew up. After 'a long time,' Judah had not fulfilled his pledge; Tamar, posing as a cult prostitute, had sex with Judah (35). From the union, twins are born.

This story follows the beginning of the Joseph story and his conflicts with his brothers. As Joseph was separated from his brothers, so Judah separated himself. Once again, we have a protest against primogeniture. However, while Joseph, the second youngest of his brothers, would rule over his brothers as he dreamed, it is Judah, the fourth born, who will be progenitor of the kings of Israel. The second of Tamar's twins, Peretz, is the father of Jesse, the father of David.

Earlier themes from the Jacob story are repeated here: Judah is deceived and twins are born. As Jacob and Rebecca deceived Isaac and Jacob was deceived by Laban, so Judah, who was deceived by Jacob about Joseph (27.26f.), is deceived by Tamar. The sexual theme is continued in the next chapter with Joseph and Potiphar's wife.

The house of David is descended from two widows, Tamar and Ruth, neither of whom was an Israelite – interesting, given the hostility to mixed marriage throughout the Bible.

JOSEPH

The final series of Genesis narratives involve Joseph as the main character, in conflicts with his brothers and father. Jacob, that master of conflicts, sets the stage by favoring Joseph over his other sons. As if this wasn't enough, he sends him to report on their work with the flocks.

- Joseph blithely tells his brothers of his dream of the sheaves who symbolically bowed down to him, and a second dream of stars and sun and moon, in which they and their parents bowed down to him. Not surprisingly, his brothers were angry with him. In fact, they hated him. When they saw him approaching on his spying mission, they determined to do away with him. Some sought to kill him while Reuben sought to save him. Judah suggested selling him to a passing caravan of Ishmaelites/Midianites. They told Jacob that Joseph was killed by a savage beast, thus gaining revenge on both their brother and their father (37).

Was Reuben's effort to save Joseph and return him to Jacob an act of reconciliation for having sex with Bilhah? Perhaps Judah's plan to prevent Joseph's death was compensation for his affair with Tamar and his future role as the progenitor of the Israelite kingdom.

Famine brought Joseph's brothers to Egypt for food, where Joseph confronted them. It is not surprising that he exacted a measure of revenge, or that the conflict continued.

- Joseph accused them of being spies and ordered all but one to prison. Then he reversed his order, demanding that they bring their youngest brother, Benjamin, to him in Egypt; that may be seen as retribution against his father, whose favoritism caused his own difficulties. Joseph might have been expected to communicate with his father once he was freed from prison and made Viceroy of Egypt. That he had not is further evidence of his hostility toward his family.

Joseph had a moment of weakness and tears when he heard his brothers express their regret for what they did to him. He sent them home after imprisoning Simeon and returning their money hidden in their bags. That gesture frightened them.

For his part, Jacob was outraged that they sought to return with Benjamin:

"My son must not go down with you" (42). The famine in Canaan remained severe so they had no choice but to return to Egypt for food knowing they could not return without Benjamin. Jacob finally acquiesced. His pain was evident: "…if I am to be bereaved of Benjamin, I shall be bereaved" (42.14).

How sad for this little old man, with a glorious role in subsequent history, but thwarted in his daily existence from his youth on.

When Joseph saw Benjamin,

"…he hurried out, for he was overcome with feeling toward his brother and was on the verge of tears; he went into (another) room and wept there" (43.3).

One would have thought that by this time Joseph would have worked through his conflicts with his family by causing them so much pain. But he was not through. His anger was not yet assuaged.

- He instructed his servant to put his silver goblet in Benjamin's bag. After the brothers left to return to Canaan, Joseph's servant intercepted them and discovered the cup. Joseph then insisted that Benjamin remain behind as his slave. Listen to the irony:

"only he in whose possession the goblet was found shall be my slave; the rest of you go back in peace to your father" (44.17).

Judah appeals to Joseph in a moving speech, concluding,

"…when (Jacob) sees that the boy is not with us, he will die…" (44.31).

What we find in the 'Joseph and his brothers' novella is that, in human relations, love is unpredictable, arbitrary, and at times, unjust. Judah, of all the brothers, understood this. Once again his father favors one son, Benjamin, over the others; although this is a painful reality, Judah is reconciled out of filial piety and love. His entire speech is motivated by the deepest empathy for his father (44.18-34). He understands how bound up the old man's life is with his youngest son. This was in spite of Jacob's saying:

"You know that my wife bore me two sons" (44.27),
as though Leah was not his wife and the other ten not his sons. Twenty-two years earlier, Judah stood by with his brothers as they presented Joseph's bloodied tunic to their anguished father. Now he will do anything – even to remaining behind as Joseph's slave in place of Benjamin – rather than see his father suffer that way again (44.30-34).

At Judah's words, Joseph breaks down again, this time before his brothers:

"His sobs were so loud that the Egyptians could hear..." (45.2). Now he tells his brothers not to be distressed: this was all part of God's plan! He then invites them to return to Canaan and bring their whole clan to Egypt. (45.9f.)

Only when he had exacted sufficient retribution from his brothers and father had his conflict with them been resolved.

Genesis ends with Jacob's blessing and testament of his sons and grandsons. First, he wishes to bless Joseph's sons, Manasseh and Ephraim. Jacob will adopt them to round out the twelve tribes since Levi's sons would become the landless tribe of priests. Now Jacob was blind (48.10) as his father had been blind when Jacob went to him for Esau's blessing. With his right hand, he purposely blesses Ephraim, the younger, thereby favoring him over the older. It's another protest against primogeniture, and the carrying out of the old conflicts. Though Joseph protested, Jacob insisted. He was willful to the end. Joseph would also be favored to the end by having a double portion of tribes over his brothers (48.12-20).

As Jacob was about to die, he assembled his sons for his final testament. Even now old conflicts were not forgotten or forgiven. Reuben, who bedded his concubine, Bilhah, though his first-born, is portrayed as "unstable as water, you will no longer excel...you brought disgrace – my couch he mounted" (49.4).

Judah, the youngest of Leah, would be the leader of his brothers and the nation (49.8-10).

Jacob, living a life of conflict and frustration, was never happy or fulfilled. He was the favorite of his mother and the younger of two brothers. His eldest sons disappointed him. He assigned the future of his people to Judah, to the fourth son of his first wife.

These stories dialectically point out tensions, expressed through a variety of conflicts.

- There first is the tension between the divine plan and the disorderly character of actual historical events, between the divine promise and the appearance that it is unfulfilled.
- The other is a tension between God's will, His providential guidance, and human freedom, the refractory nature of man.

In Genesis, we find a complex moral and psychological realism. God's purposes are always entrammeled in history because they are dependent on the acts of individual men and women for their realization. The biblical characters, in their fictionalized form, are multifaceted and contradictory, exhibiting their clear conflicts.

Conflict is a major theme throughout Genesis. In the early, sacred chapters, the conflict is between God and rebellious humans, from Adam and Eve on. The narratives about the Patriarchs and their families are for the most part, secular. These stories serve to tell of the origins of the Israelites and what God expected of them. However, they are primarily concerned with family complexity and conflicts. They may be seen as a cautionary warning to later generations of what to avoid in their relationships with one another.

Chapter Five

The Book of Exodus is succinctly summarized. The author points out that since Israelites are not mentioned in Egypt's historical wealth, it, for the most part, is a fictional account. He infers that its worth lies in its holding Israelites together as a nation.

EXODUS

Exodus changed the Israelites: no longer an extended family, they became a nation. Exodus is essentially a sacred work; God and the greatest of the prophets, Moses, are its central figures.

After four hundred years of slavery in Egypt, the people had been freed through the ten plagues brought by God against their masters. Those plagues with the death of his son finally led Pharaoh to allow them to depart under the leadership of Moses.

While Moses provided human leadership, God was involved with the Israelites until they reached the Promised Land. God not only called Moses to his role as leader and caused the plagues, he destroyed the Egyptian army at the Reed Sea, led the Israelites for forty years through the wilderness, assured them military victories against their enemies, fed them miraculously with quail and manna, and through Moses at Mt. Sinai revealed the Torah to them. Torah was to become the centerpiece of their identity.

While the events of Exodus are detailed as historical narratives, they are historic fiction told to impart important values. There is no historical material in Egyptian sources to indicate that the Israelites were in Egypt.

It's possible that there are bits of history embedded in Exodus. Egypt with its agricultural resources, even in time of famine, would draw outsiders in their times of need. Genesis has both Abraham and Jacob's family sojourning in Egypt.

The essential ideas of Exodus are these:

- there is a single God who is all-powerful and who maintains the covenant which he made with Abraham;
- God will perform miracles for his people so that his purposes for them will be fulfilled;
- there is always hope, even after four hundred years of slavery, that freedom will come.

Another major theme is the rebelliousness of the Israelites, who constantly complain about the hardships of their sojourn, its lack of security, and sparse food and water. Their lack of appreciation reached a peak when they worshiped a golden calf while Moses was on Mt. Sinai receiving the revelation from God.

This is great theater! God and Moses, paired up against a massive opposition. Everything in the narratives is exaggerated to establish God as powerful, and Moses as his faithful servant: an unappreciated, long-suffering leader of a recalcitrant people. Moses, a prince in Pharaoh's palace, sacrificed all to answer God's call to lead his chosen people. To add insult to injury, Moses was not allowed to enter the Promised Land. He had to settle for seeing it in the distance before his death.

Exodus is basically a faith document focusing on a central and crucial series of events that resulted in Israel's becoming a nation. Its paramount theses are God's law to guide and his power to save and protect Israel.

Following the conquest by Babylonia in 586, this faith was particularly important. This importance grew some seventy years later with the return of some of those exiles. In Judaea, the community had to rebuild Jerusalem and the Temple. Belief in the power of God and his concern for Israel served the secular purpose of reinforcing their ability to survive as a community.

Therein lay another lesson for those who governed the society: Exodus details five rebellions of the people against God and Moses. If the Israelites could be so disloyal and difficult toward God and his prophet, the rulers should not be surprised that governing would be troublesome for them as well. The history of the monarchy would forcefully bear this out.

Chapter Six

Prior to discussing the third section of the Pentateuch, it seems apropos to present an overview of my distinction between pre-exilic [586 BC] and post-exilic [500 **BC**] Israel. Before the conquest by Babylonia in 586, late-stage Judaean monarchy and Israelite society was similar to other regional cultures. The prophets, its various ideologues, perceived that the end of the monarchy was imminent; they became convinced that a strong reconstituted monarchy was unlikely in the immediate future. Their view of Israel changed radically. As will be noted in my chapters on history and the prophets, incremental steps in this direction had been taken. Israel, with its center for the sacrificial cult in Jerusalem, would no longer be constituted as a nation-state like others with a centralized government (monarchy). From being an essentially secularized society with a cultic center and many localized altars, it became a sacralized society with a single sanctuary in Jerusalem controlled by the priesthood, with God as the power validating it.

Once there was a secular Bible within the Bible: the Bible of the post-exilic period was made into a sacred collection of books. In the process of editing the pre-exilic material, many of the secular accounts had sacredness infused into them (like yeast through a lump of dough). I contend that the concept of God's central role of universal being, as the one deity over all of nature and peoples, originated with the Prophet Amos. He viewed God as the One in charge of the history of all nations. While Israelite society was predominantly polytheistic throughout the pre-exilic period, the idea of a single all-powerful God gradually infused Judaean society and became its central belief and binding ideology. Isaiah of the Exile was the major force in completing the work of Amos who had lived 200 years before him. Increasingly, scholars of the Hebrew Bible have become convinced that the exile and its threat to the survival of Israel was the major motivation behind the additions to earlier secular materials - as well as the writings of the post-exilic prophets and the other books of this period. There were two elements in this development: that God was THE deity to whom total loyalty was demanded; and that the physical expression of this loyalty was the rebuilt Temple in Jerusalem. There the sacrificial cult would be continued. Their future was to be glorious: Israel would eventually triumph and all people would recognize their God as THE God.

The essential ideological elements were the belief in the all-powerful God, coupled with Israel as God's special servant chosen for a glorious mission. That mission was to spread the knowledge of God, and the demands of God, to all humanity.

In his brief synopsis of Leviticus,
the author employs a few passages
indicating tis innate secularity.

LEVITICUS

The book of Leviticus may be seen as a sacralized book par excellence. It contains the institutions and philosophy, which ultimately shaped Israel's national and religious existence. These include laws, the priesthood, the forms of Temple worship, and the tribal foundation of society. All of these are formulated in the narrative regarding the Tabernacle where the cult was performed during the Exodus. Rituals for purification and exculpation were seen as aspects of the same concern.

Leviticus is obsessed with holiness and purity. All of the actions of ordinary living were sacralized. God's involvement was seen everywhere: wrongs could be set right through proper rituals.

- laws of sacrifices cover seven chapters;
- the consecration of priests, two;
- laws regarding the clean and unclean, five;
- and those laws which would govern a holy people, ten.

Laws which were essentially secular in their pre-Exile origins were set into a holy framework. As redacted after the Exile, they were to be followed because of God's commandments. Governance by a human king was replaced by the governance of the Levites, God's selected priests who received God's laws directly as they had been revealed to Moses and by him to the people.

Leviticus' laws touch upon every matter of concern to priest and person. A few of these are:

o (Lev.11. 1-20) This is the case with the very involved and detailed laws regarding food:

"And the Lord spoke to Moses and Aaron, saying to them: speak to the people of Israel, saying: From all the land animals, there are creatures which you may eat."

o (11.3-47) The remainder of the chapter offers details of what is allowed and disallowed.

o (chapters 13 and 14) Laws of impurity (tzarat) relate to a variety of skin diseases and their treatment as well as what seems to be mold and mildew as they affect buildings, building materials and fabrics.

o (14.54-57) "This is the ritual for any skin disease: for an itch, for eruption-diseases in clothing and houses, and for a swelling or an eruption or a spot, to determine when it is unclean or clean. This is the ritual for such diseases".

o   (15.31-33; 1-30) A similar situation is found regarding impurity resulting from bodily discharges such as semen, menstrual fluid, a discharge due to gonorrhea or urethral infections: "Thus you shall keep the people of Israel separate from their uncleanness, so that they do not die in their unceanness by defiling my tabernacle that is in their midst. This is the ritual for those who have a discharge: for him who has an emission of semen, becoming unclean thereby, for her who is in the infirmity of her period, for anyone, male or female, who has a discharge, and for the man who lies with a woman who is unclean".

These fundamentally secular laws were placed within a sacred framework for their enforcement. All laws were to be obeyed because they were God's laws and were incumbent upon his people who were to be holy.

- (19. 1-2) "The Lord spoke to Moses, saying: Speak to the congregation of the people of Israel and say to them: You shall be holy, for I the Lord your God am holy";
- (22. 31-33) "Thus shall you keep my commandments and observe them: I am the Lord. You shall not profane my name, that I may be sanctified among the people of Israel: I am the Lord; I sanctify you, I who brought you out of the land of Egypt to be your God: I am the Lord".

Chapter Seven
A continuation of Exodus

NUMBERS

This book continues the sacred history begun in Exodus. Its major concern is with Israel's march to its final destination, the Promised Land. While Israel is bonded by its covenant with God, its rebellions are recounted. Because of these rebellions, all of those in the exodus, with the exception of Joshua and Caleb, are to die before entering Canaan. A new generation born in freedom will enter in their place.

Having been led by Moses they will have developed faith in their faithful God who will fulfill the promises he made to their ancestors. **Numbers** is primarily concerned with:

- Maintenance of the cult;
- purity of their camp;
- the role of the Levites;
- the sacrificial laws and their expiatory efficacy.

Aside from secular laws, Numbers is overwhelmingly sacred in nature, but there are several secular episodes.

- o (27.1-11) In the story of Zelophehad's daughters, we learn that women have the right to inheritance when there are no male heirs.
- o (35.9-34) Cities of refuge are described for those who commit accidental homicide and there are laws concerning those who commit intentional homicide.

Chapter Eight

*The author employs Deuteronomy
to reinforce his conclusion that the
Bible was originally secular but
made was made sacred after the
exile in order to turn Israelites into
a united nation able to survive.*

DEUTERONOMY

Book Five of the Pentateuch, Deuteronomy, completes the sacred accounts of TORAH. Deuteronomy restates many laws and experiences of the four previous books. It may also be called the Second Law, as it reaffirms the covenant, repeating what the people are to do – based on their special relationship to God. Although God is the supreme ruler of everything, Israel is intimately related to God.

Two features stand out in this book:
> **(1)** Sacrifices are to be offered in only one place: (12.13-14) "Take care that you do not offer your burnt offerings at any place you happen to see. But only at the place the Lord will choose in one of your tribes – there you shall offer your burnt offerings and there you shall do everything I command you."
> This is in complete contrast to God's earlier telling them that they

may sacrifice:
- (Exodus 20.24) "in every place where I cause my name to be remembered I will come to you and bless you".
- (Genesis 12. 7-8) It had been legitimate for Abraham to sacrifice at Shechem and Bethel;
- (Gen. 35. 1-2) Jacob at Shechem;
- (1 Samuel)Samuel at several sites;
- (1 Kings 18. 20-46) Elijah on Mt. Carmel.

The gross idolatry in the last decades before 586 was the likely rationale for this edict, and for Josiah's attempt to centralize the cult in Jerusalem. In addition to purifying the cult, it served to consolidate political power in the monarchy and the power of the Jerusalem priesthood over that of the priests of outlying sanctuaries.

> **(2)** Deuteronomy also reinforced and made central the concept of retributive justice:

- o (11.26-28) "See, I am setting before you today a blessing and a curse: the blessing, if you obey the commandments of the Lord your God that I am commanding you today; and the curse, if you do not obey the commandments of the Lord your God, but turn from the way that I am commanding you today…".
- o (16.20) The guiding light to the laws found in Deuteronomy is: "Justice, justice you shall pursue, so that you may live and occupy the land that the Lord your God is giving you".

While Deuteronomy was set historically as Israel was about to enter the Promised Land and included the laws required to succeed there, it was actually written as Israel was about to enter another, more threatening period: the eve of their exile after the Babylonian conquest. To help insure their survival, the power of God and his special relationship with Israel were reinforced. To avoid being absorbed into Babylonian culture – as the ten northern tribes had been absorbed when exiled to Assyria – the Judaeans had to be convinced that they were still tied to an all-powerful God who would protect and care for them as long as they remained loyal to him. In Deuteronomy, justice (not mercy) is featured. God would deal justly with them as long as they dealt justly with others, especially their fellow Judaeans as long as they obeyed God completely – to the exclusion of any other deity.

Chapter Nine

Here it is postulated a step-by-step
developmental process the Laws
went through.

LAWS OF THE PENTATEUCH

Every human community develops ways to live together in peace and harmony. Long ago, when these groups were small – not much more than a collection of families -- laws typically were informal, given orally, and memorized by practice.

Family groups formed into clans then into tribes, causing their laws to gradually assume a formal structure. Their codes were early on enforced through group pressure, and then by men in positions of authority. Individuals' knowledge of those laws and their judicious character were hallmarks of their authority.

As tribes consolidated into city-states and then nations, legal codes were formulated. They were typically named for the kings in whose reigns these codes were defined, and who, not coincidentally, had the power to enforce them. The earliest of these codes known to us is dated about 2050 and is attributed to Ur Nammu, the king of Sumer and Akkad. The best-known formulation is that of Hammurabi, 1728-1686, who ruled Babylonia.

Our Biblical society went through a similar process. Scholars have identified several different law codes imbedded within the Pentateuch. While there is considerable disagreement on the details of these codes, there is agreement that they developed gradually, over centuries.

The earliest of these codes is the Book of the Covenant, which broadly includes Exodus 19.1-24.11 but more particularly 20.22-23.33. Closely related to this code is 34.10-28. This 'book' is usually dated from the tribal period, or from the early monarchy.

These statutes are denoted as those laws Israel was to keep in accord with the covenant made with God. They were formulated in a terse, judicial style; in these laws, God addresses Moses.

The second formulation, the Deuteronomic, was obviously found in Deuteronomy. It is dated about 621; it was said to have been discovered when the Temple of Jerusalem was being cleaned and renovated at the command of King Josiah (2 Kings 23.2). It was then read at the request of the king (2 Kings 23.2).

The Deuteronomic Code may be seen as a revision of the Covenant Code; material had been added to conform to the ethical sensitivity of the reform movement inaugurated by King Josiah. It was to be read aloud every seven years (Deut.31.10f.).

In its formulation, Moses addresses the people in God's name. The people are told ten times to love God. The only capital punishment is by stoning.

The last legal formulation, the Priestly Code, is usually dated from the exilic or post-exilic periods, from 586-450. It includes material from Exodus 25 through Numbers 10, with scattered passages in Genesis. It has a substratum, Leviticus 17-26, called the Holiness Code because of its emphasis on holiness

> "You shall be holy, for I the Lord your God am holy" (Lev. 19.2).

The Priestly Code, while later than the others, includes a great deal of material that was already ancient when assembled before 450. While it differs from the earlier codes in many ways, it also has much in common with them:

- ➢ it calls for the dignity and purity of the family;
- ➢ strict justice in the courts;
- ➢ rights of the stranger and the poor;
- ➢ prohibitions against murder, robbery, incest, and adultery.
- ➢ Those faithful to the code are to fear God.
- ➢ Burning and stabbing are added as punishment for capital offenses.

In reading through these codes, one is struck by the conflation of civil and criminal law with laws relating to the Temple, the priesthood and the sacrificial cult. This was not unusual in legal codes of the Middle East.

The Pentateuch, as we have inherited it, is a thoroughly sacred collection of books in structure and intent. It seems to have been edited during or shortly before the time of Ezra, the scribe-priest who lived in the middle of the fifth century. It was he who read the whole Torah to the assembled congregation of exiles returned to Jerusalem (Nehemiah 8.2).

Though the Torah was not completed until the fifth century, there was an awareness of it as the embodiment of God's law centuries before:

o   In the mid-eighth century, the prophet Hosea stated:

"I will write for him (Ephraim) my Torah" [law] (Hosea 8.12).

o   Two passages by the Deuteronomist also attest to this usage: "and Moses wrote this Torah…" (Deut. 31.9).

o   and "…Joshua wrote these words in the book of the Torah of God.." (Joshua 24.26).

o   About 520 the prophet, Haggai wrote: "Thus said the Lord of hosts: 'ask the priests for a ruling (Torah)…' " (Haggai 2.11).

The word Torah may be translated as 'law' or 'instruction' or 'teaching' or 'direction.'

What is clear is that even before it was completely codified, the society had a definite concept of God as the law-giver. God gave that law to the people through the mediation of Moses on Mt. Sinai. Laws developed over centuries that were secular in nature and intent, were then included in this corpus of law. The law was accepted as divine. That added to its value with God in the role of ultimate Enforcer and Guarantor of his people's well-being.

Secular laws cover virtually every aspect of life, personal and societal. A representation of the laws will follow in chronological order.

COVENANT CODE (Exodus)

- "Whoever strikes a person mortally shall be put to death. If it was not premeditated, but came about through an act of

God, then I will appoint for you a place to which the killer may flee" (21.12f.).

- "Whoever strikes father or mother shall be put to death. Whoever kidnaps a person, whether that person has been sold or is still held in possession, shall be put to death. Whoever curses father or mother shall be put to death" (21.15-17).

- "If any harm follows (in an action), then you shall give life for life, eye for eye, tooth for tooth, hand for hand, foot for foot, burn for burn, wound for wound, stripe for stripe" (21.23-25).

- "If someone steals an ox or a sheep, and slaughters it or sells it, the thief shall pay five oxen for an ox, and four sheep for a sheep" (22.1).

- "If a thief is found breaking in, and is beaten to death, no bloodguilt is incurred; but if it happens after sunrise, bloodguilt is incurred" (22.2f.)

- "You shall not permit a female sorcerer to live. Whoever lies with an animal shall be put to death" (22.18f.).

- "You shall not wrong or oppress a resident alien, for you were aliens in the land of Egypt. You shall not abuse any widow or orphan" (22.21f.).

- "You shall not spread a false report. You shall not join hands with the wicked to act as a malicious witness. You shall not follow a majority in wrongdoing; when you bear witness in a lawsuit, you shall not side with the majority to pervert justice; nor shall you be partial to the poor in a lawsuit" (23.1-3).

DEUTERONOMIC CODE (Deuteronomy)

- "A woman shall not wear a man's apparel, nor shall a man put on a woman's garment..."(22.5).

- "You shall not plow with an ox and a donkey yoked together. You shall not wear clothes made of wool and linen woven together" (22.10f.).

- "A man shall not marry his father's wife, thereby violating his father's rights" (23.1).

- "When a man is newly married, he shall not go out with the army or be charged with any related duty. He shall be free at home one year, to be happy with the wife whom he has married" (24.5).

HOLINESS CODE (Leviticus) a.k.a Priestly Code

o "When you reap the harvest of your land, you shall not reap to the very edges of your field, nor gather the gleanings of your harvest. You shall not strip your vineyard bare, or gather the fallen grapes of your vineyard; you shall leave them for the poor and the alien..."(19.10f.).

o "You shall not steal; you shall not deal falsely; and you shall not lie to one another" (19.11).

o "You shall not defraud your neighbor; you shall not steal; and you shall not keep for yourself the wages of the laborer until morning. You shall not revile the deaf or put a stumbling block before the blind... "(19. 13f.).

o "You shall not eat anything with its blood. You shall not practice augury or witchcraft" (19.26).

o "You shall not cheat in measuring length, weight, or quantity. You shall have honest balances, honest weights, an honest ephah, an honest hin..."(19.35f.).

The Ten Commandments are emblematic of the blended nature of the sacred and the secular. The first four are sacred, featuring the nature of God and banning idolatry, while the last six call for the honoring of parents and injunctions against murder, adultery, stealing, bearing falsewitness and coveting (Exodus 20.1-17; Deuteronomy 5.6-21).

Chapter Ten

Sorting out the contradictions and contributions of individual historians has been one of the major preoccupations of biblical scholars for more than a century. In this book, the emphasis is on the secular nature of the society. But it notes the sacred orientation that the historians and prophets found to be necessary for survival of the Jews, following the Babylonian conquest and exile and the subsequent Persian domination of the area.

THE HISTORIES

The discipline of history is essentially secular. The Oxford English Dictionary calls history "a narrative of past events."

It may also be defined as studies of past individuals and groups of people, interacting with one another in relationships of various kinds within a given socio-politico-economic environment - as affected by its geographical setting and material culture.

An essential part of understanding history lies in recognizing the ideologies present in a society and the ideologies of its historians. Some historians of Biblical society had a sacred or religious orientation in which God (or gods) or other spiritual factors were seen as determining the course of human events.

The histories of the Hebrew Bible – Joshua, Judges, Samuel, Kings, Chronicles, Ezra and Nehemiah, – were completed between 630 and 400. During this period, the very existence of the Jewish people was in danger. These historians recast historical records and oral traditions into a sacred interpretation of history. The Jews were seen as having a special covenanted relationship with God, and to the land of Israel, the Davidic monarchy, and the Temple in Jerusalem. Royal and other archival materials were utilized by these historians but were reframed with an overarching sacred interpretation.

There is considerable consensus that the first six historical books have a common orientation from the author(s) of Deuteronomy. This development is thought to have occurred in two stages:

- late in the reign of King Josiah (640-619);
- and early in the exilic period, after 586.

The major ideological elements of Deuteronomic Historians include:

- the exclusive worship of God;
- the disastrous consequences of idolatry;
- the central role of the Temple and its priests in Jerusalem;
- and the supremacy of the Davidic dynasty.

Later works, Chronicles, Ezra and Nehemiah, are usually dated to the fifth century, and are primarily concerned with the:

- returning exiles;
- reconstruction of the Temple;
- and reinstitution of the sacrificial cult.

Some contemporary scholars believe that the historical accounts of the Hebrew Bible are at best theocratic or quasi-historical. But a sounder conclusion is that: with careful study, secular history may be extracted from the biblical texts. Furthermore, many of the sacred elements of the histories served secular ends, such as the survival of an embattled people. In this analysis, the secular denotes those activities in which events are determined by human action, while the sacred defines events determined by divine action and miracles.

Like monarchs and other officials of other ancient Near Eastern kingdoms, Israelite kings maintained written records of their reigns. Various biblical passages refer to written chronicles, such as:

- o "the annals of the kings of Judah" (1 Kings 14:29; 15:7, 23; 22:46);
- o "the annals of the kings of Israel-Ephraim" (1 Kings 14:19; 15:31; 16:5, 14, etc.);
- o and "the annals of the kings of Judah and Israel" (2 Chron. 16:11; 25:26; 27:7; 28;26, etc.).

There were also:

- o "the records of David" (1 Chron. 29:29);
- o "the book of the acts of Solomon" (1 Kings 11:41; 1 Chron. 9:29);
- o the records of the deeds of Rehoboam which had been written by Shemaiah the prophet and Iddo the seer" (2 Chron. 12:15; cf. 13:22);
    - o and a work of Jehu the son of Hanani that recounted the history of Jehosphaphat's reign and was incorporated into "the books of the kings of Israel" (2 Chron. 22:34).

The written collections called
> "the book of the wars of Yahweh" (Num. 21:14) and "the
> book of Yashar" (Josh. 10:12; 2 Sam. 1:17)

included material attributed to the premonarchic period and point to transmission of this material during the monarchy. Scribes were used to preserve records:

- ❑ by the monarchy (2 Sam 8:16; 1 Kings 4:3; Prov. 25:1; Ps. 45:1);
- ❑ the army (2 Kings 25:19, Jer. 52:25; cf. Josh. 18:9; Judg. 8:13-17);
- ❑ and the judicial administration (Jer. 32:11-14).
- ❑ the priesthood also had scribes specializing in the storage of legal material through writing (Jer. 8:7-8).

Much of the Bible records the history of ancient Israel and its people. Its historical record is central to Israel's developing its identity, its past, its future, and its relationship with God. While expansively-based on oral traditions, and official records, the Hebrew Bible, as we have received it, is, to a broad degree, an ideologically guided text. Because it developed over a very long time during variable circumstances, style and message variations abound within it.

In addition, the writing of Biblical history was effectively utilized, for ideological and communal purposes, as a vehicle to enhance the survival of the Jewish people. It, in particular, led Judaeans from having an identity as a nation state into a people whose identity rested in its religion.

Chapter Eleven

*Secular accounts of the conquest of
the Promised Land by Joshua are
separated from the miraculous
intervention of God.*

JOSHUA

Verifiable Biblical History begins with the book of Joshua; it contains
known cities, locations, states, routes and likely king-names. It, however,
is the least of the Bible's histories, being structured as a sacred book with
God serving as the major war leader who guides and supports Joshua as he
did Moses.

The book has two major purposes: **(1)** reinforce the message of
Deuteronomy regarding obedience to God, **(2)** and the rapid, complete
conquest of the land promised by God.

>   The Israelites' responsibility was to obey God and worship him
alone:

> "Every place where you set foot is yours: I have given
> it to you as I promised Moses...as I was with Moses, so I will
> be with you...Be strong, be resolute; observe diligently all the
> law which my servant Moses has given you...Then you will
> prosper and be successful in all that you do" (1.3,5,6,7,8).

> "(Joshua said)...it was the Lord God himself who
> fought for you...the Lord your God himself drove them out
> for your sake...observe and perform everything written in the
> book of the law of Moses, without swerving to the right or
> left...But the same Lord God...can equally bring every kind
> of evil on you..." (23.3,4,6,15).

The conquest was seen as complete after all the inhabitants had been
annihilated:

> "So Joshua defeated the whole land, the hill country and the
> Negeb and the lowland and the slopes, and all their kinds; he
> left no one remaining, but utterly destroyed all that breathed,
> as the Lord God of Israel commanded. And Joshua defeated
> them from Kadesh Barnea to Gaza, and all the country of
> Goshen, as far as Gibeon. Joshua took all these kings and their

land at one time, because the Lord God of Israel fought for Israel" (Joshua 10:40-42).

In one sense, the book of Joshua is an extended sermon on the power of God, his loyalty to the Israelites and their obligation to worship only him. Its purpose was to steel the people against whatever dangers were to confront them. It is clear from archeological research that the conquest was not as described in Joshua. The places named in the book have been identified and no pattern of destruction can be correlated with this period. The Israelites settled in new villages in the unoccupied central highlands, not in rebuilt Canaanite strongholds.

Indeed, in several Joshuan passages, the conquest is seen as less than complete with many, if not most, Canaanites surviving:

- "Now Joshua was old and advanced in years; and the Lord said to him, 'You are old and advanced in years, and very much of the land still remains to be possessed' " (13.1).
- "But the people of Judah could not drive out the Jebusites; so the Jebusites live with the people of Judah in Jerusalem to this day" (15.63).
- "They did not, however, drive out the Canaanites who lived in Gezer: so the Canaanites have lived in Ephraim to this day but have been made to do forced labor" (16.10).

Sacred history obscures what had most likely been a gradual conquest in order to indicate the power of God and the reward the people gained from their loyalty to him.

Joshua is portrayed as Moses' appropriate successor, and his career parallels much of what Moses did. Both had miraculous crossings of water, Moses of the Reed Sea and Joshua of the Jordan; both sent out spies and apportioned the Promised Land; the accounts of both reflected a unified people, an ideal which was never achieved except briefly during the reigns of David and Solomon.

God's miracles in Joshua's time included the conquest of Jericho, and the stopping of the sun in Gibeon and the moon at Aijalon (10.2). The miracle of the toppling of the walls of Jericho has God as the hero (6.1-24).

A possibly secular account of spies sent to search out the land, especially Jericho, has the agents assisted by a prostitute, Rehab, when a report of their presence came to the king of Jericho. She saved them by hiding them and then misdirecting the king's soldiers.

While Rehab acknowledges the presence of God, the story makes sense with the divine intervention left out (2.1-24). She and her family were then rewarded by being rescued and taken to the Israelites' camp before "they burned down the city and everything in it" (6.22-25).

While archeologists have determined that Jericho could not have been destroyed at this time, this story may reflect a secular account of the conquest of a nearby town, conflated into God's miraculous assistance in the conquest of a well-known major city.

A similar process may have been at work with the conquest of Ai.

In the secular account, Joshua sends spies ("Joshua sent men from Jericho to Ai…and said to them, 'Go up and spy out the land'") who miscalculate the strength of its inhabitants. After sending relatively few troops, they were forced to flee on being challenged by the men of Ai (7.2-5). A new strategy was devised, an ambush, which led to the defeat of Ai (8.3-7a, 8a, 9-17,19-29). As is the wont of the historian of Joshua, God is given full credit:

> "Then the Lord said to Joshua, 'Stretch out your sword that is
> in you hand toward Ai; for I will give it into your hand.'"
> (8.18; 1, 2, 7b, 8b).

Other secular elements include tribal conflicts over the allotment of apportioned land, possibly reflecting later intertribal dissension (17.1-17).

Also noted is the technological superiority of the Canaanites who possessed "chariots of iron" which prevented the Israelites defeating them (17.18).

Chapter Twelve

*It is held that Judges set the stage
and provisioned the justification for
Israel to become a monarchy in
order to end pervasive idolatry and
immorality.*

JUDGES

Like Joshua's[2], the book of Judges may also be seen as an extended sermon with two major themes.

(1) Judges' first theme is a cyclic history. (Judges 2.11-19) After being disloyal to God by worshipping idols, the Israelites were defeated by their neighbors. In regret, the people then cried out to God, who sent them a Judge, a military leader, who would defeat their enemies. But once again the people reverted to idolatry and were again conquered; the cycle continued.

(2) Its second major theme is its call for a dynastic king who would bring to an end idolatry and immorality. This is summarized in the last verse of the book: (21.25, also 17.6; 19.1)

> "In those days there was no king in Israel; everyone did as he pleased."

Clearly, what they did was wrong and the establishment of a monarchy was essential.

There also is a sub-theme to the contrary: that a monarchy was not only unnecessary but uncalled for since God was the true king. This theme is continued in the first chapters of I Samuel.

Let us here consider some background factors influencing the history incorporated into Judges:

> Israelite tribes were not unified;
> Tribal elders led them;
> Priests in local shrines served them.
> These leaders were not adept at protecting their communities that were periodically overcome by their neighbors.
> The complaint about idolatry refers to the Israelites' over-adapting to the culture of their neighbors, threatening their special identity.

---

[2] An extended sermon stating that God is the ruler of the Israelites and they are to obey him fully in order to gain success and prosper.

Those favoring monarchy may be seen as modernizers recognizing that new political and military arrangements were necessary for their protection and survival. Tribal elders, the old elite opposed such a dramatic change since they would lose their power in the process. Judges delineates the first step in establishing a monarchy: the culmination of that process is described in the books of Samuel. Judges depicts the secular monarchists opposed to the traditional elites and priests, but that conflict was essentially a secular one: figuring out how this disparate group of tribes could be united as a political and military force that could repulse attacks from their militant neighbors.

Apart from occasional interpolations and introductions by Deuteronomic historians, little evidence is presented regarding Israelite cultic practices. Mention is made, however, of a number of cultic centers at Shechem, Bethel, Gilgal, Shiloh, Bochim and Ophrah. Judges' varied activities were carried out in a secular manner to meet the threat of neighboring peoples.

These judges may be divided into two groups: minor and major.

Concerning the former, there is little information other than their names, families and length of service (10.1-5; 12.8-15).

Among them are Tola of Issachar and Jair of Gilead (Manasseh); Izban of Bethlehem, Elon of Zebulun and Abdon of Ephraim.

As was true of all of the judges, they were said to judge [or rule] over a limited territory and to deliver all of Israel – this latter claim is clearly an exaggeration. They and the other, better-known judges, dealt with attacks from nearby neighbors; they typically responded like leaders of the individual tribes and clans.

Assorted reasons are offered for the failure to complete the conquest during the time of Joshua. They include:

- technological inadequacy ("The Lord was with Judah, so he took possession of the hill country; but they were not able to dispossess the inhabitants of the plain, for they had iron chariots [1.19].")
- The historian offers a secular explanation here while offering a sacred one later:

"These are the nations that the Lord left so that He might test
by them all the Israelites who had not known any of the wars
of Canaan, so that succeeding generations of Israelites might

be made to experience war...(neighboring enemies) served as a means of testing Israel, to learn whether they would obey the commandments which the Lord had enjoined upon their fathers through Moses" (3.1-4).

The major judges had greater and better-known successes. These include:

Othniel who defeated King Cushan-rishathaim of Aram and brought peace for forty years (3.7-11);

Ehud of Benjamin defeated Moab after slaying its king, Eglon, through stealth (3.12-30);

Deborah was both a prophetess and judge. She worked with Barak, possibly a military figure, to lead Naphtali and Zebulun against King Jabin of Canaan and his general, Sisera (4 and 5).

Jephtah led Gilead (a part of Manasseh) against Ammon. The Ephraimite challenge against Jephtah, when Jephtah failed to seek their assistance, indicates something of the lack of unity among the Israelite tribes. That failure led to a war between them, with 42,000 Ephraimites reportedly slain (11-12.7).

Those conflicts typically represent God as being involved. But they may also be seen as secular conflicts. As the Israelites gradually consolidated their possession of parts of Canaan, they were frequently – and effectively -- challenged by their neighbors. While their defeats were seen by the Deuteronomic historians as the result of their disloyalty to God, they were, rather, the result of their lack of military and political skills.

The chapters devoted to Gideon testify to the importance of his career in defeating the threat of the Midianites. The Gideon material sets the stage for the establishment of the monarchy as narrated in the books of Samuel. Both books reflect both sacred and secular orientations in regard to the establishment of a monarchy. On the one hand, Gideon refuses the offer to become king and to begin a dynastic monarchy; for him, God is the ruler. This is evidence of the continuing power of the old elites. Gideon's evil son, Abimelech, who asserts himself as king and meets an ignoble death, reinforces this anti-monarchical viewpoint.

There are, at the same time, clear indications that Gideon was himself an idolater and that his society was infused with alien practices. These necessitated the institution of a strong secular regime to restore worship of the one true God. This is a projection back into earlier history of a belief on the part of the Israelites in a single, all-powerful God.

To demonstrate the power of God in Gideon's war against Midian, God had him reduce his army of 32,000 to 10,000 and then to 300:

"And the Lord said to Gideon, 'You have too many troops with you for Me to deliver Midian into their hands; Israel might claim for itself the glory due to me, thinking, "Our own hand has brought us victory"'" (7.2-8).

As a result of his amazing victory over the Midianites, killing upwards of 135,000 (8.10-12),

"Then the men of Israel said to Gideon, 'Rule over us – you, your son, and your grandson as well; for you have saved us from the Midianites.' But Gideon replied, 'I will not rule over you myself, nor shall my son rule over you; the Lord alone shall rule over you'" (8.22-23).

But of course, someone or some group would have to rule as God's representative(s) and this would mean that the old elites would be replaced by a king. Reinforcing this negative response to the establishment of a monarchy is the story of Gideon's son, Abimelech.

After killing seventy of his brothers with only one escaping, he was proclaimed king by the people of Shechem. The people turned against him after he ruled for three years. During a battle, as Abimelech approached a tower, a woman dropped a millstone, wounding him severely. He asked his servant to deliver a coup de grace so that it would not be said that he had been killed by a woman (9).

While the editors of the text present the idea that Israelite society continued to believe in the one true, all-powerful God described in Genesis 1, the reality of a thoroughly polytheistic society is also obvious. Gideon himself was an idol worshipper. He had his people contribute their booty from the Midianites to make an idol of God (8.24-27). (This story may have been the model for the Golden Calf events at Sinai (Exodus 32.2-4).)

Earlier in the Gideon narrative, the author depicts Gideon as obedient to Yahweh, building an altar to him and destroying one to Baal, which had been erected by his father. Given the fact that his father was a worshiper of Baal, it is not surprising that Gideon's original name was

Jerubbaal which could mean 'he who contends for Baal' rather than, as the text has it, 'Let Baal contend with him, since he tore down his altar' (6.23-32).'

The pro-monarchic tradition of Judges presents an even more dramatic series of events to support the need for a king to end intolerable cultic practices and idolatry. Micah, an inhabitant of the hill country of Ephraim, had an image sculpted and another image refined. He also had an ephod, a priestly garment, (it also adorned cult statues) and teraphim (statues or figurines representing household gods) and made one of his sons his priest.

The author of this story was presenting further evidence for the religious anarchy of the time and the necessity for a king:

"In those days there was no king in Israel; every man did as he
pleased." (17.6).

Shortly thereafter, a young man from Bethlehem in Judah, a levite, left home, looking for a job. Micah hired him and he became his cohane [priest]. Since Micah had assigned first his son and then a wandering levite as his priest, it is likely that levites at this time were simply members of a religious guild rather than the Levites who descended from the tribe of Levi and continued their priestly role through the sons of Aaron (17).

The next chapter begins with the mantra:

"In those days there was no king in Israel ..."

This introduction was intended to prepare the reader for an even more dramatic argument for a king. The tribe of Dan, after being expelled from their territory, passed into the hill country of Ephraim and stopped near the house of Micah. When they learned that Micah owned numerous idols, the men of Dan then insisted that the levite join them together with those idols:

"Come with us and be our father and priest. Would you rather
be priest to one man's household or be priest to a tribe and
clan in Israel?" "The priest was delighted. He took the ephod,
the household gods, and the sculptured image, and he joined
the people" (18).

What we seem to have here is an argument for the monarchy, for secular rule, with the implication that a king would insure that the abuses of idolatry would be ended.

The book of Judges ends with the 'outrage at Gibeah.' A concubine left her husband to return to her father. Her husband followed her to force her return to him. He left with her and lodged on the way back with a man of Gibeah in Benjamin. That evening, several men of the town called for the guest to be sent out so that they could have sex with him. The host then offered his virgin daughter and the concubine in his place.

It was the concubine who was finally sent out. Abused and raped all night by the men of the town, she died shortly after being deposited at the host's home. When her husband returned home, he cut her body into twelve pieces and distributed them throughout Israel. The Benjaminites would not hand over the evil-doers; the tribe of Benjamin was attacked and 25,000 of them were killed (19-21).

This secular story begins and ends with the mantra, 'In those days when there was no king in Israel…(19.1; 21,25).' Clearly, it was essential that there be a dynastic monarchy in Israel so that idolatry and moral outrages of this kind could be stopped. Ending idolatry and immorality reinforced the necessity of having a king as a way to protect the Israelites' territory.

Chapter Thirteen

*SAMUEL is viewed from both a secular and a
sacred perspective. Some emphasis is given
into examining the effect on the priesthood on
being delegitimized upon a monarchy being
inaugurated.
How Kings Saul and David rose and ruled are
compared.*

SAMUEL

The two books of Samuel detail the eleventh century decline in the role
and power of Israel's priestly class with the institution of a monarchy. Its
first kings, Saul and David, are the lead characters of I Samuel. The book
of Samuel is, in its intents and purposes, a continuation of Judges, a book
that was written, in part, to prove the necessity for establishing a
monarchy.

Literary analysis shows that the books of Samuel went through an
extensive process of development. Form analysis implies that these books
include extracts from many sources. This process is clear from duplicated
stories and contradictory accounts of its central characters.

Governance of Israel, prior to the monarchy, was shared among the tribal
elders, the judges and the priests. The purpose of the monarchy was to end
rampant idolatrous practices as well as immoral communal and individual
behavior, and to maintain a military force to protect Israelite tribes from
their neighbors, particularly the Philistines.

In this period leading to the establishment of a monarchy, we know
of only two major priests, Eli and Samuel. They were probably
representative of priests whose roles extended beyond just offering
sacrifices in sanctuaries.

Samuel-the-prophet also served as a judicial figure with a military
role as well, although the nature of that role is not totally clear. Although
Samuel, the priest-prophet, initially rejected the demand for a king, he
finally acquiesced by first anointing Saul, and then David.

Instituting a monarchy radically changed the traditional infrastructure of
their priesthood. There must have been great resistance not only from the
priests who correctly perceived that they would be dominated but also

from the traditional elites and the tribes; they desired a unifying military figure, but not one who would be too controlling.

1-Samuel's first section demonstrates how inadequate their priesthood was for defeating enemies. It also details the immoral activities of the priests. It is because David finally established his dynasty after Saul's opposition and death that Saul is generally denigrated while David is glorified. As is to be amplified upon, David's dynasty is to be eternal, as God noted in proposing the building of the Temple and in promising that the Messiah would come from his bloodline. David becomes the very model of a great king. The passages glorifying him are not difficult to identify. Many other sections that appear to be historical balance them.

Narratives, particularly about David, seem to be based on a combination of oral and written traditions, and on royal records. Later historians, especially Deuteronomists [DH], because of their general theological orientation, did some rewriting making God the author of history.

They involved the deity in many accounts so as to reinforce the importance of God in a time when there was no monarchy, or only a very weak, ineffectual king. Many passages, where God is **the** force, may be better understood by simply leaving out phrases like "*God said...*" or "*God did...*" Large portions of the books of Samuel are fundamentally secular, with sacred allusions clearly being added later.

From about the period of the Exodus down to David's time, the socio-geography of the Middle East was being shattered by the "Sea-peoples". About 1175, the Philistines (a Sea-peoples tribe) threatened the Israelites. These Philistines originated as Aegean peoples who having been driven from Crete and the shores of Asia Minor, were forced to sail the sea south. On failing to penetrate Egypt, those refugees turned to South Canaan's seacoast, conquering territories by employing superior military and political organizations. They gradually moved inland, bringing pressure on the Israelite tribes. The Philistines were technologically advanced, with a metallurgical monopoly of technology for manufacturing implements and weapons [especially of a new metal, iron].

Concerning that monopoly, Samuel instructs us:
"Now there was no smith to be found throughout all the land
of Israel; for the Philistines said, 'The Hebrews must not make

swords or spears for themselves'; so all the Israelites went
down to the Philistines to sharpen their plowshare, mattocks,
axes, or sickles; The charge was two-thirds of a shekel for the
plowshares and for the mattocks, and one-third of a shekel for
sharpening the axes and for setting the goads. So on the day of
the battle neither sword nor spear was to be found in the
possession of any of the people with Saul and Jonathan, but
Saul and his son Jonathan had them," (I Samuel 13.19-22).

For economic reasons alone, the need for a military leader was apparent.

Added to their lack of military ability, the priests were delegitimized
because of their immorality. While Eli, the lead-priest of Shiloh, was
acceptable to the people, his successor-sons were not.

"Now the sons of Eli were scoundrels; they had no regard for
the Lord or for the duties of the priests to the people…thus the
sin of the young men was very great in the sight of the Lord;
for they treated the offerings of the Lord with contempt (I
Samuel 2.12f.; 17; cf. 2.13-16; 22-25).

Being immoral and disloyal to God made them unsavory to the faithful but
what ended their political favor was that they were bad commanders. The
Philistines defeated the Israelites while being command by priests. Those
idolaters even captured the Ark of the Covenant. Some 34,000 Israelites
were killed; among the dead were Eli's sons, Hophni and Phinehas (4.1-
11). Even the presence of the Ark of the Covenant could not help the
Israelites in this conflict.

While Eli's sons were evil, his protégé, Samuel was quite different.
God spoke to Eli:

"I will raise up for myself a faithful priest, who shall do
according to what is in my heart and in my mind" (2.35).

Samuel seems to have served a rather large territory: it's span went from
his home in Ramah and the major shrine in Shiloh; he traveled the circuit
from Bethel to Gilgal and Mizpah (7.15-17).

But as with Eli's sons so were Samuel's:

"Yet his sons did not follow in his ways, but turned aside
after gain; they took bribes and perverted justice" (8.3).

The sacred leadership was thus ineffective and corrupt:

"Then all the elders of Israel gathered together and came to
Samuel at Ramah, and said to him, 'You are old and your sons

do not follow in your ways; appoint for us a king to govern us,
like the nations.'" (8.4f.).
After Samuel appealed to God, he agreed when God noted that the people
had rejected God not Samuel.

    Samuel warned the people of the material and personal cost of a
monarchy, but they insisted, once again saying:

"...we are determined to have a king over us, so that we may
be like other nations, and that our king may govern us and go
out and fight our battles" (8.6-22).

As a result, religious leaders had been set-aside for secular leaders. While
the remainder of the books of Samuel include elements of the cult and
priesthood, secular leaders were now in control.

While the cult and the religious leaders might bring a bit of unity to the
people, the text clearly indicates that society saw a need for political
change.

    The people had learned from the example of their neighbors that a
militarily-adept secular ruler was essential for their survival. Religious
authorities would still have a role in society, but it would be far more
limited than that Eli and Samuel apparently once held.

The Philistine incursions may be seen as the motivating factor that brought
about this change, but they were really just its precipitating element.
Israelite society was growing in size and substance. The nation now faced
the necessity for protecting, and possibly of enlarging, its territory.
Traditional religious leaders could not provide the organization of a
powerful monarch or his skills.

    There would, of course, be opposition from the traditional elites.
both personal and tribal, as well as others who must oppose a king.

    In a later time when the society was structured religiously for its
survival, a necessity would arise to protect the role of God. For this
reason, God's directions were interspersed into secular documents, which
comprise the bulk of the books of Samuel. This, in retrospect, became
essential when the monarchy was destroyed in 586, when the role of God
and the priesthood again regulated Israelite society.

SAMUEL, SAUL, AND DAVID
SACRED ACCOUNTS

The two books of Samuel come from several traditions. Later editors, both from contemporary historians and from age-old oral traditions, assembled them. Religiously oriented historians, like the Deuteronomists used this material to establish and confirm the new sacred social system: God had to be depicted as the major determinant of Israelite history.

Although Samuel was to lose his political power to a king, he remained a person of stature, making and unmaking rulers, at least according to the sacred accounts.

The prophet Amos may have initiated the role of God as the author of history, the God who worked through priests and prophets, judges and kings, in the eighth century.

Israelite society, at that time, was divided into two segments: **(1)** the sacred, centering on the sacrificial cult in the Temple in Jerusalem and outlying temples, **(2)** the secular, governing society through its political leaders.

Its northern tribes never truly were unified for long. That is why they chose their first king from their smallest, presumably weakest tribe.

Following the conquest of those ten northern tribes by the Assyrians in 722, Judaean society was restructured. Various religious leaders returned God to the center of affairs so as to protect the kingdom. The northerners [the Kingdom of Israel], not possessing any such survivalist ideology, were absorbed into Assyrian society and culture, and so lost their special religious identity.

Although Deuteronomic historians now placed God in the center of the historical process, earlier historical records survive in the text. Deuteronomic historians have both Saul and David appointed by God through Samuel. Since, according to the sacred account, God selected both Saul and David, therefore David's ascendance also must be the result of God's decisions. From the sacred point of view, God chose Saul, but the secular account describes him as selected because he was from a minor family of the smallest tribe. Saul's decline is attributed to **(1)** his failure to kill all of the Amelekites as God had instructed, and **(2)** because of his offering of sacrifices in the absence of the priest, Samuel.

In this sacred version, David appears righteous in that twice he could have killed Saul but declined to do so while Saul attempted, on several occasions, to kill David. The historical, secular account portrays Saul as having little real political and military power as well as owning a problematic personality. His ultimate failure was his defeat and death in battle with the Philistines. David then gained control over the kingdom but only after a prolonged war against Saul's successors.

SAUL and DAVID:
SECULAR ACCOUNTS?

Saul, a young man from the tribe of Benjamin, goes to the priest for help in seeking some lost donkeys (9.1-14).

Prior to Saul's arrival, God instructs Samuel:

"Tomorrow at this time I will send to you a man from the land of Benjamin, and you shall anoint him to be ruler over my people Israel. He shall save my people from the land of the Philistines; for I have seen the suffering of my people, because their outcry has come to me" (9.16-17).

"Samuel took a vial of oil and poured it on his head, and kissed him; he said, 'The Lord has anointed you ruler over his people Israel. You shall reign over the people of the Lord and you will save them from the hand of their enemies all around'" (10.1).

Within this account the sacred and the secular seem to mingled:

"As for your donkeys that were lost three days ago, give no further thought to them, for they have been found. And on whom is all Israel's desire fixed, if not on you and on all your ancestral house? Saul answered, 'I am only a Benjaminite, from the least of the tribes of Israel, and my family is the humblest of all the families of the tribe of Benjamin. Why then have you spoken to me in this way'" (9.20-21).

While this is included in the sacred version, it would also make secular sense: having a king was an innovation for the society as a person from the smallest tribe would appear to be less threatening and less likely to exploit the others.

Saul might also have been selected because of his appearance:

"He had a son whose name was Saul, a handsome young man. There was not a man among the people of Israel more handsome than he; he stood head and shoulders above everyone else" (9.2).

Another passage describes Saul as at least reticent about being anointed king, this time in public:

"Then Samuel brought all the tribes of Israel near, and the tribe of Benjamin was taken by lot. He brought the tribe of Benjamin near by its families, and the family of the Matrites was taken by lot. Finally he brought the family of the Matrites near man-by-man, and Saul the son of Kish was taken by lot. But when they sought him, he could not be found. So they inquired again of the Lord, 'Did the man come here?' and the Lord said, 'See, he has hidden himself among the baggage.' Then they ran and brought him from there. When he took his stand among the people, he was head and shoulders taller than any of them. Samuel said to all the people, 'Do you see the one whom the Lord has chosen? There is no one like him among all the people.' And all the people shouted, 'Long live the king!'" (10.20-24).

Both anointing episodes indicate reluctance on Saul's part to be king, while his behavior indicates a defect in his personality. Also indicative of this are the following parallel passages, probably based on the same tradition:

- "After that you shall come to Gibeath-elohim, at the place where the Philistine garrison is; there, as you come to the town, you will meet a band of prophets coming down from the shrine with harp, tambourine, flute, and lyre playing in front of them; they will be in a prophetic frenzy. Then the spirit of the Lord will possess you, and you will be in a prophetic frenzy along with them and be turned into a different person" (10 5-6).

- "As he turned away to leave Samuel, God gave him another heart; and all these signs were fulfilled that day. When they were going from there to Gibeah, a band of prophets met him; and the spirit of God possessed him, and he fell into a prophetic frenzy along with them. When all who knew him before saw how he prophesied with the prophets, the people said to one another, 'What has come over the son of Kish? Is Saul also among the prophets?' A man of the place answered, 'And who is their father?' Therefore it became a proverb, 'Is Saul also among the prophets?' When his prophetic frenzy had ended, he went home" (10.9-13).

- "Then Saul sent messengers to take David. When they saw the company of the prophets in a frenzy, with Samuel standing in charge of them, the spirit of God came upon the messengers of Saul, and they also fell into a prophetic frenzy. When Saul was told, he sent other messengers, and they also fell into a frenzy. Saul sent messengers again the third time, and they also fell into frenzy. Then he himself went to Ramah. When he came to the great well that is in Secu, he asked, 'Where are Samuel and David?' And someone said, 'They are at Naioth in Ramah.' He went there, toward Naioth in Ramah; and the spirit of God came upon him. As he was going, he fell into a prophetic frenzy, until he came to Naioth in Ramah. He too stripped off his clothes, and he too fell into a frenzy before Samuel. He lay naked all that day and all that night. There it is said, 'Is Saul also among the Prophets?'" (19.20-24).

Saul was known to be mentally disturbed; music therapy was recommended:

"Now the spirit of the Lord departed from Saul, and an evil spirit from the Lord tormented him. And Saul's servants said to him, 'See now, an evil spirit from God is tormenting you. Let our lord now command the servants who attend you to look for someone who is skillful in playing the lyre; and when the evil spirit from God is upon you, he will play it, and you will feel better.' So Saul said to his servants, 'Provide for me someone who can play well, and bring him to me.' One of the young men answered, 'I have seen a son of Jesse the Bethlehemite who is skillful in playing, a man of valor, a warrior, prudent in speech, and a man of good presence; and the Lord is with him.' So Saul sent messengers to Jesse, and said, 'Send me your son David who is with the sheep.' Jesse took a donkey loaded with bread, a skin of wine, and a kid, and sent them with his son David to Saul. And David came to Saul, and entered his service. Saul loved him greatly, and he became his armor-bearer. Saul sent to Jesse, saying, 'Let

> David remain in my service, for he has found favor in my sight.' And whenever the evil spirit from God came upon Saul, David took the lyre and played it with his hand, and Saul would be relieved and would recover, and the evil spirit would depart from him" (16.14-23).

Saul later suffered from paranoia regarding David, although this may have been at least in part justified by what David did – or what Saul thought he did.

Part of the sacred account may be found in Samuel's justification of his career:

> "He said to them, 'The Lord is witness against you, and his anointed is witness this day, that you have not found anything in my hand.' And they said, 'He is witness.'" (12.5; 12.1-25) This chapter restated the Deuteronomic formula of obeying God for success and recounting all that God had done for them since the exodus from Egypt.

Because Saul and his successors failed to establish a dynasty, or defeat the Philistines, the sacred account had to have God delegitimize them in two episodes.

(1) While Saul was with his troops ready to confront the Philistines, his army wavered. To encourage them, Samuel was to offer a sacrifice on their behalf to God. Samuel was late and the troops were dispersing, so Saul offered up the sacrifice.

> "Samuel then said to Saul, 'You have done foolishly; you have not kept the commandment of the Lord your God, which he commanded you. The Lord would have established your kingdom over Israel forever, but now you kingdom will not continue; the Lord has sought out a man after his own heart; and the Lord has appointed him to be ruler over his people, because you have not kept what the Lord commanded you'" (13.13-14).

One could argue that this is a highly contrived reason for such drastic action, particularly when Samuel himself showed up late.

(2) The other deciding event came when Samuel indicated to Saul that God wanted the Amelekites totally destroyed for their opposing the Israelites on their passage during the Exodus. Saul won the battle, but spared their king, Agog, and the best of their livestock. Once again, the penalty was harsh:

> "The word of the Lord came to Samuel: 'I regret that I made Saul king, for he has turned back from following me, and has not carried out my commands.' Samuel was angry; and he cried out to the Lord all night" (15.10-11).

"For rebellion is no less a sin than divination, and stubbornness is like iniquity and idolatry. Because you have rejected the word of the Lord, he has also rejected you from being king" (15.23).

> Apparently God, in choosing Saul as king, did not select wisely.

In the sacred account, God immediately moved to select Saul's successor, though he had several years of rule remaining:

> "The Lord said to Samuel, 'How long will you grieve over Saul? I have rejected him from being king over Israel. Fill your horn with oil and set out; I will send you to Jesse the Bethlehemite, for I have provided for myself a king among his sons.' Samuel said, 'How can I go? If Saul hears of it, he will kill me.' And the Lord said, 'Take a heifer with you and say, 'I have come to sacrifice to the Lord''" (16.1-2).

None of Jesse's sons would do except the one who wasn't there, David.

> "He sent and brought him in. Now he was ruddy, and had beautiful eyes, and was handsome. The Lord said, 'Rise and anoint him; for this is the one.' Then Samuel took the horn of oil, and anointed him in the presence of his brothers; and the spirit of the Lord came mightily upon David from that day forward. Samuel then set out and went to Ramah" (12-13).

It is after this anointing that David joins the court of Saul to provide music and serve in Saul's military (16.14-23).

> Another element in delegitimating Saul as king was his behavior toward David. Saul persistently attempted to kill him or have him killed, ostensibly because of David's military success and his popularity with the general populace:

> "David went out and was successful wherever Saul sent him; as a result, Saul set him over the army. And all the people, even the servants of Saul, approved. As they were coming home, when David returned from killing the Philistine, the women came out of all the towns of Israel, singing and

dancing, to meet King Saul, with tambourines, with songs of joy, and with musical instruments. And the women sang to one another as they made merry, 'Saul has killed his thousands, and David his ten thousands.' Saul was very angry, for this saying displeased him. He said, 'They have ascribed to David ten thousands, and to me they have ascribed thousands; what more can he have but the kingdom?' So Saul eyed David from that day on. The next day an evil spirit from God rushed upon Saul, and he raved within his house, while David was playing the lyre, as he did day by day. Saul had his spear in his hand; and Saul threw the spear, for he thought, 'I will pin David to the wall.' But David eluded him twice" (18.5-16).

Saul also sent him into battle against the Philistines but David survived brilliantly:

"Now Saul's daughter Michal loved David. Saul was told, and the thing pleased him. Saul thought, 'Let me give her to him that she may be a snare for him and that the hand of the Philistines may be against him.' Therefore Saul said to David a second time, 'You shall now be my son-in-law.' Saul commanded his servants, 'Speak to David in private and say, 'See, the king is delighted with you, and all his servants love you; now then, become the king's son-in-law.' So Saul's servants reported these words to David in private. And David said, 'Does it seem to you a little thing to become the king's son-in-law, seeing that I am a poor man and of no repute?' The servants of Saul told him, 'This is what David said. Then Saul said, 'Thus shall you say to David, 'The king desires no marriage present except a hundred foreskins of the Philistines, that he may be avenged on the king's enemies.' Now Saul planned to make David fall by the hand of the Philistines. When his servants told David these words, David was well pleased to be the king's son-in-law. Before the time had expired, David rose and went, along with his men, and killed one hundred of the Philistines; and David brought their foreskins, which were given in full number to the king, that he might become the king's son-in-law. Saul then gave him his daughter Michal as a wife. But when Saul realized that the

Lord was with David, and that his daughter Michal loved him, Saul was still more afraid of David. So Saul was David's enemy from that time forward" (18.20-29).

David had the opportunity to kill Saul twice but demurred each time; some thought that God brought about this reluctance. In this account, Saul acknowledges David's righteousness, and that his succession to the throne is by the will of God:

"When David had finished speaking these words to Saul, Saul said, 'Is this your voice, my son David?' Saul lifted up his voice and wept. He said to David, 'You are more righteous than I; for you have repaid me good, whereas I have repaid you evil. Today you have explained how you have dealt well with me, in that you did not kill me when the Lord put me into your hands. For who has ever found an enemy, and sent the enemy safely away? So may the Lord reward you with good for what you have done to me this day. Now I know that you shall surely be king, and that the kingdom of Israel shall be established in your hand'" (24.16-20).

A similar situation is described in 26 where David again declines to take advantage of Saul's vulnerability. These sacred accounts keep God involved directly and indirectly in charge of the events described. Because of the roles David served for later Israelite history and ideology, particularly in proposing the building of the Temple in Jerusalem, and in the fact that the messiah would come from his lineage, the sacred interpolations by Deuteronomic historians [the DH] always placed David in a favorable light.

The secular accounts of Saul point out some of Saul's successes against the Philistines.

"Saul chose three thousand out of Israel; two thousand were with Saul in Michmash and the hill country of Bethel, and a thousand were with Jonathan in Gibeah of Benjamin; the rest of the people he sent home to their tents. Jonathan defeated the garrison of the Philistines that was at Geba; and the Philistines heard of it. And Saul blew the trumpet throughout all the land, saying, 'Let the Hebrews hear!'"(13.2-4).

"When Saul had taken the kingship over Israel, he fought against all his enemies on every side – against Moab, against the Ammonites, against Edom, against the kings of Zobah, and against the Philistines; wherever he turned he routed them. He did valiantly, and struck down the Amalekites, and rescued Israel out of the hands of those who plundered them" (14.47-48).

Saul had mixed roles which undoubtedly diluted his purely secular office as king: his functions as an ecstatic prophet, and as a priest.

But as a general, he had no standing army and had to rely on volunteers when battle was to take place. As a monarch, he had no capital, no taxing system, and no bureaucracy to support him. So he continued to farm:

"When the messengers came to Gibeah of Saul, they reported the matter in the hearing of the people; and all the people wept aloud. Now Saul was coming from the field behind the oxen; and Saul said, 'What is the matter with the people, that they are weeping?' So they told him the message from the inhabitants of Jabesh" (11.4-5).

Technologically, his forces were far inferior to those of the Philistines. As a result, Saul failed in his primary responsibility: to defeat the enemies of Israel, particularly, the Philistines. After a major defeat by the Philistines, Jonathan and two of his brothers were killed; Saul was mortally wounded and took his own life:

"Now the Philistines fought against Israel; and the men of Israel fled before the Philistines, and many fell on Mount Gilboa. The Philistines overtook Saul and his sons; and the Philistines killed Jonathan and Abinadab and Malchishua, the sons of Saul. The battle pressed hard upon Saul; the archers found him, and he was badly wounded by them. Then Saul said to his armor-bearer, 'Draw your sword and thrust me through with it, so that these uncircumcised may not come and thrust me through, and make sport of me.' But his armor-bearer was unwilling; for he was terrified. So Saul took his own sword and fell upon it. When his armor-bearer saw that Saul was dead, he also fell upon his sword and died with him.

So Saul and his three sons and his armor-bearer and all his men died together on the same day. When the men of Israel who were on the other side of the valley and those beyond the Jordan saw that the men of Israel had fled and that Saul and his sons were dead, they forsook their towns and fled; and the Philistines came and occupied them. The next day, when the Philistines came to strip the dead, they found Saul and his three sons fallen on Mount Gilboa. They cut off his head, stripped off his armor, and sent messengers throughout the land of the Philistines to carry the good news to the houses of their idols and to the people. They put his armor in the temple of Astarte; and they fastened his body to the wall of Beth-shan. But when the inhabitants of Jabeshgilead heard what the Philistines had done to Saul, all the valiant men set out, traveled all night long, and took the body of Saul and the bodies of his sons from the wall of Beth-shan. They came to Jabesh and burned them there. Then they took their bones and buried them under the tamarisk tree in Jabesh, and fasted seven days" (31.1-13).

According to the text, Saul had reluctantly accepted the monarchy, and was never appreciated. His reign was troubled affording him little, if any, recorded achievement or satisfaction.

The accounts of David noted thus far are a part of the sacred views: David was selected by God and was righteous and honorable, particularly in comparison to Saul. This bias continues to glorify David.

However, the books of Samuel include much that appears to be historical and essentially secular. David could not have been as popular as has been indicated; he was the ruler only of Judah until he defeated the forces of Saul's successors after engaging in a seven and a half year armed conflict with them. This conflict foreshadowed the hostilities between the northern and southern tribes following Solomon's reign.

Chapter Fourteen

Herein is continued 1 Samuel's story of Saul and
David with more emphasis given to David's negative
aspects. The author suggests that Saul hated David
because he suspected David of an affair with his son,
Jonathan. David's conspiracy with the Philistines is
another black mark tarnishing his subsequent
glorification by Deuteronomic historians.
This is followed by a detailed listing of the secular
events of King David's reign provided by 2 Samuel.

David

The various traditions regarding David make it difficult to answer every question arising from the text. In it David is glorified as an attractive, brave, and successful warrior, a man generally admired by the people of Saul's kingdom. He was specifically appointed by God to succeed Saul whom God determined to be disobedient, and therefore unworthy to found a dynasty. Another unattractive aspect to Saul is that he did not reciprocate David's loyalty to him; in fact, Saul attempted to kill, or have him killed. David, on the other hand, having opportunities to kill Saul, did spare him.

It is hypothesized that later Israelite editors added these sacred formulations to the secular accounts of David's accomplishments so as to purposefully glorify him. While David had some military successes, the adulation of him was far less widespread than narratives indicate.

Secular accounts seem to be based on historical records, and on oral traditions developing around a very attractive and compelling personality. The many negative aspects of David's personality and career may have been preserved in part to prevent his being idealized, or even worshipped. Biblical society, constantly influenced by idolatry, injected or preserved negative accounts of its major heroes, so that only God was deemed worthy of worship.

Two further sacred accounts of David's exploits ought to be cited.

(1) The community of Keilah was under attack by the Philistines and David's troops feared to engage them. David therefore inquired of God, who answered him:

> "Yes, go down to Keilah; for I will give the Philistines into your hand. So David and his men …fought with the Philistines…and dealt them a heavy defeat…" (23.4f.).

(2) On another occasion when David had the opportunity to kill Saul, and was encouraged to do so by his troops, he refused:

> "The men of David said to him: 'Here is the day of which the Lord said to you, "I will give your enemy into your hand, and you shall do to him as it seems good to you.' Then David went and stealthily cut off a corner of Saul's cloak. Afterward David was stricken to the heart because he had cut off a corner of Saul's cloak. He said to his men, 'The Lord forbid that I should do this thing to my lord, the Lord's anointed, to raise my hand against him; for he is the Lord's anointed.' So David scolded his men severely and did not permit them to attack Saul. Then Saul got up and left the cave, and went on his way." (24.4-7).

Later, we read:

> "When David had finished speaking these words to Saul, Saul said, 'Is this your voice, my son David?' Saul lifted up his voice and wept. He said to David: 'You are more righteous than I; for you have repaid me good, whereas I have repaid you evil. Today you have explained how you have dealt well with me, in that you did not kill me when the Lord put me into your hands'" (16-19).

In addition to these sacred accounts, there are several other glorification narratives. The best known is his challenge to the giant Philistine, Goliath, who was well armed and armored, while David carried just a slingshot:

> "So David prevailed over the Philistine with a sling and a stone, striking down the Philistine and killing him; there was no sword in David's hand. Then David ran and stood over the Philistine; he grasped his sword, drew it out of its sheath, and killed him; then he cut off his head with it" (17.50-51).

However, the killing of Goliath is elsewhere attributed to another:

> "Then there was another battle with the Philistines at Gob where Elhanan son of Jaare-oregim the Bethlehemite, killed Goliath the Gittite, the shaft of whose spear was like a weaver's beam" (2 Samuel 21.19).

Secular, historical accounts sketch a different portrait. That David was attractive to men as well as women is attested to by his relationship with

Jonathan. Not only was David the husband of Saul's daughter, Michal, but he had a special tie with Saul's son, Jonathan. The king's son seems to be expressing his love for David, by giving him his royal apparel and weapons, symbols of his authority:

"When David had finished speaking to Saul, the soul of Jonathan was bound to the soul of David, and Jonathan loved him as his own soul. Saul took him that day and would not let him return to his father's house. Then Jonathan made a covenant with David, because he loved him as his own soul. Jonathan stripped himself of the robe that he was wearing, and gave it to David, and his armor, and even his sword and his bow and his belt" (18.1-4).

When Jonathan learned that Saul was again seeking to have David killed, Jonathan warned David: "Saul spoke with his son Jonathan and with all his servants about killing David. But Saul's son Jonathan took great delight in David (and warned him):

'My father Saul is trying to kill you...'" (19.1f.).

After Jonathan pleaded with Saul in behalf of David, David returned to the court, with Saul noting that David was not to be put to death (19.4-7).

Once again Saul plotted to have David killed; this time, he was saved by his wife, Michal (19.8-17).

When David asked Jonathan why Saul was determined to kill him, he said that he would find out. The narrative concludes with these words:

"Jonathan made David swear again by his love for him; for he loved him as he loved his own life" (20.17; 1-17).

That Saul was suspicious of the relationship between Jonathan and David is clear when Saul responded to Jonathan's defense of David:

"Then Saul's anger was kindled against Jonathan. He said to him, 'You son of a perverse, rebellious woman! Do I not know that you have chosen the son of Jesse to your own shame, and to the shame of your mother's nakedness? For as long as the son of Jesse lives upon the earth, neither you nor your kingdom shall be established. Now send and bring him to me, for he shall surely die'" (20.30-31).

On the day following Saul's threat, Jonathan went to meet David in order to report on the events at the court. This passage seems to allude to a sexual encounter, the last between Jonathan and David:

"David arose out of a place toward the south, and fell on his face to the ground, and bowed down three times; and they kissed one another, and wept with one another until David 'higdeel.'" (20.41).

Higdeel is the Hebrew causative verb 'to be large.' Could it mean that David had an erection?

After Jonathan is slain, David laments his death with these words:

"I am distressed for you, my brother Jonathan; very pleasant have you been to me; wonderful was your love for me, passing the love for women (2 Samuel 1.26).

Interestingly, the text never has David use 'love' for any of his wives. Was David's love for Jonathan reciprocal, or was it a manipulative attempt to gain advantage and protection in the court of Saul? David's lament would indicate that their love was true.

Belying David's high status, popularity and his glorification in the sacred accounts, many passages indicate the opposite. His followers were a motley group:

"Everyone who was in distress, and everyone who was in debt, and everyone who was discontented gathered to him; and he became captain over them. Those who were with him numbered about four hundred." (22.2; 600 are noted in 23.13).

At this point, it is clear that David appealed only to society's riff-raff, the marginalized who were rejected by the at-large-community.

He apparently had so little support among his own people that he entrusted his parents to the king of Moab (23.3)

He then extorted animals and other goods from Nabal, a Calebite in the north. Refusing David's threats, Nabal asked:

"Who is David? Who is the son of Jesse? There are many servants today who are breaking away from their masters" (25.10).

Nabal soon died and David took his widow, Abigail, as a wife (25.2-42).

When David hid from Saul in the south in the territory of the Ziphites, they reported his location to Saul (26.1f.).

A most compelling indication of David's plight and insecurity is his turning to the Philistines to escape from Saul. Upon arriving at Gath and before facing its king, Achish, David was willing to degrade himself by feigning madness:

"David took these words to heart and was very much afraid of King Achish of Gath. So he changed his behavior before them; he pretended to be mad when in their presence. He scratched marks on the doors of the gate, and let his spittle run down his beard. Achish said to his servants, 'Look, you see the man is mad; why then have you brought him to me? Do I lack madmen, that you have brought this fellow to play the madman in my presence? Shall this fellow come into my house?" (21.12-15).

"David said in his heart, 'I shall now perish one day by the hand of Saul; there is nothing better for me than to escape to the land of the Philistines; then Saul will despair of seeking me any longer within the borders of Israel, and I shall escape out of his hand.' So David set out, with the six hundred men who were with him, went over to King Achish son of Maoch of Gath. David stayed with Achish at Gath, he and his troops, every man with his household, and David with his two wives, Ahinoam of Jezreel, and Abigail of Carmel, Nabal's widow" (27.1-4).

David remained there for sixteen months, and was given a city to control and use as a base for raiding nearby tribes:

"David left neither man nor woman alive to be brought back to Gath, thinking, 'They might tell about us, and say, David has done so and so." Such was his practice all the time he lived in the country of the Philistines. Achish trusted David, thinking, 'He has made himself utterly abhorrent to his people Israel; therefore he shall always be my servant." (27.11-12).

Most dramatic was David's willingness to join Achish in a campaign against the forces of Saul:

"In those days the Philistines gathered their forces for war, to fight against Israel. Achish said to David: 'You know, of course, that you and your men are to go out with me in the army'" (28.1-2).

The leaders of Achish's army who did not trust David saved David from joining the Philistines in their battle against Israel. Although David protested his loyalty to Achish, Achish acquiesced to his officers:

> "David said to Achish, 'But what have I done? What have you found in your servant from the day I entered your service until now, that I should not go and fight against the enemies of my lord the king?' Achish replied to David, 'I know that you are as blameless in my sight as an angel of God; nevertheless, the commanders of the Philistines have said, 'He shall not go up with us to the battle. Now then rise early in the morning, you and the servants of your lord who came with you, and go to the place that I appointed for you. As for the evil report, do not take it to heart, for you have done well before me. Start early in the morning, and leave as soon as you have light.' So David set out with his men early in the morning, to return to the land of the Philistines. But the Philistines went up to Jezreel" (29.8-11).

It is possible that the editors of this account found it too unsavory to have David actually join the Philistines in the battle that defeated Israel with the killings of Saul and Jonathan.

Once the Israelite forces had been routed by the Philistines, and both Saul and Jonathan were dead, David quickly and systematically moved towards building and consolidating his power. David led the tribe of Judah to defeat the remnants of Saul's forces. These, however, remained a military threat long after David was established as king over the twelve Israelite tribes. Rebellions led by his son, Absalom, and the Benjaminite, Sheva against David, indicate that the northern, non-Judahite tribes, had not fully acquiesced to David's rule. David and his regime had not completely consolidated their control.

David's successor, Solomon, appears to have had a peaceful reign, but the splintering of David's nation after Solomon's death indicated an ever-present north-south split.

Second Samuel is basically a secular continuation of First Samuel. Sacred interpolations by DH maintain its ideology of God, God who is involved in historical processes. In that way, purely human power-conflicts and politics would appear to be divinely ordained and inevitable, leading to an eternal Davidic dynasty.

The secular nature of 2-Samuel is demonstrated by the mention of God in the first chapter, where its references to God are

- "people of the Lord" (12)
- "The Lord's Anointed" (14, 16), referring to Saul.;
- In other chapters the hand of DH is clear: the Ark of God is brought to Jerusalem,
- David proposes building a permanent Temple for God;
- God assures that his kingdom will last forever (6.1-29).
- The secular account of Absalom's rebellion against David and his subsequent death is noted as the result of God taking vengeance on David's enemies and saving him (18. 19, 28, 31).
- Similarly, Absalom's selecting Hushai's advice over Ahitophel's, leading to David's survival, is seen as God's action (16.18; 17.14).

With few other exceptions, the remaining events in this book are related in a secular mode. They're what might be expected in the conflicts between power-blocs represented by David's forces and those of Saul's descendants. The true monarchy, having been divinely chosen and repeatedly supported by God, as interpreted by DH (shadowy in 1-Samuel) is more fully established in 2-Samuel.

The episodes recounted in this book indicate that while David had some military success in Saul's army, he never gained the widespread following alleged in his glorification accounts. He was a renegade – not that surprising considering Saul's jealousy and repeated attempts to have him killed.

On becoming king David, unlike Saul, was strong enough to rule – he, possibly, had gained more followers and wealth while living with the Philistines – gathering enough wealth to become the king of Judah with a capital in Hebron where he reigned for seven and a half years (2.4, 11).

We read that, at the time, Saul's old army and political control had not disintegrated.

- ✓ Abner, the commander of Saul's army, established Saul's son, Ishbaal, as king over Israel (2.8-10a).
- ✓ There then ensued the first of many battles between the house of Saul and David, with David's army winning (2.12,17).

✓ While few battles between them are detailed, the text makes clear that "There was a long war between the house of Saul and the house of David; David grew stronger and stronger with the house of Saul becoming weaker and weaker" (3.1).

A contributing factor in Israel's weakness seems to have been dissension among its leadership.

➢ Abner sought to assert his authority by attempting to grab Saul's concubine, Rizpah, an action resisted by Ishbaal (3.6-8).

➢ Abner than sought an alliance with David, who demanded that his wife, Michal, the daughter of Saul, be separated from her then-husband and returned to David (3.12-15). This was the first of many acts by David to neutralize, or destroy, Saul's family.

➢ Abner then plotted to bring Israel over to David. Joab, probably viewing Abner as a powerful rival to him, killed Abner. David disavowed responsibility for this act and predicted a dire end for Joab and his family (3.17-39).

Keeping his pledge, David took Jonathon's crippled son, Mephibosheth, under his protection. Being crippled, he was not seen as a threat (4.4).

Saul's son and successor, Ishbaal, was then assassinated; the killers brought his head to David. Once again David protested and had the killers executed (4.5-12); that was consistent with King David's pattern of:
- disavowing responsibility;
- showing no pleasure over the deaths of possible threats;
- mourning over them is repeated over and again.

We see it demonstrated with:
- the Amelekite who put Saul out of his misery,
- with Abner,
- with Absalom.

After a prolonged conflict, the Israelites finally capitulated by going to Hebron and accepting David as their king (5.1-5). David's army then conquered Jebus, which would become his capital, Jerusalem (5.6-10). Jerusalem was a stronghold situated on a height; it was a neutral site, not having been attached to either Judah or Israel.

David continued to fight and defeat the Philistines. In two accounts, God is noted as encouraging David and guaranteeing his success (5.17-25).

As well as being their political and military center, by bringing the Ark to Jerusalem, he also established it as the cultic-religious center of the kingdom reinforcing its sacred role with the populace, (6.1-5).

David's military exploits were so successful that he established a mini-empire. He defeated the:
- ✓ Philistines;
- ✓ Moabites;
- ✓ Edomites;
- ✓ Ammonites;
- ✓ Amelekites. Then going into Syria;
- ✓ Zoba on the Euphrates River;
- ✓ Damascus (8.1-14).
- ✓ Later, Aram (Damascus) joined Ammon against Israel and both were again defeated (10.19).

His administration included Seraiah as secretary, and Joab as the head of the people's army. Benaiah led Cerethites and Pelethites mercenaries. These Greek/Philistine also served as court troops protecting David's person, and as a balance to the people's army led by Joab with whom David had differences. There were also two high priests, Zadok and Aviatar. Dividing priestly authority made each more dependent on the king (8.15-18).

The lengthy account of David and Bathsheba follows. The king saw her bathing, and had an affair with her that led to her pregnancy. David attempted to have her husband, Uriah the Hittite, return from battle to sleep with her but Uriah, out of loyalty to the troops still at the battle front, refused. David then sent instructions to Joab to engage in a battle in which Uriah was certain to be killed.

David then married Bathsheba, but the child they conceived died shortly after its birth. Their second child, Solomon, became David's successor.

Nathan, noted as a prophet, is here more appropriately seen as a royal councilor: he challenged David on his immoral actions with Bathsheba, but especially those against Uriah. While Nathan was correct that David acted immorally - a judgment with which David agreed - open acknowledgement of and remorse for his actions would resonate with the Jerusalem's general populace, which certainly knew of it. The king was not to be seen as above the law.

DH also inserts God's judgment into the narrative, foreshadowing why David spent his life at war, and why domestic feuds and difficulties would trouble the king's last years:

> "Now therefore the sword shall never depart from your house, for you have despised me, and have taken the wife of Uriah the Hittite to be your wife. Thus says the Lord: I will raise up trouble against you from within your own house; and I will take your wives before your eyes, and give them to your neighbor, and he shall lie with your wives in the sight of this very sun. For you did it secretly; but I will do this thing before all Israel, and before the sun. David said to Nathan, 'I have sinned against the Lord.' Nathan said to David, 'Now the Lord has put away your sin; you shall not die'" (12.10-13; Chapters 11 and 12).

Even though the text presents only two disputes among David's children, it may be assumed that there were many more, since he is said to have had more than twenty wives and concubines (5.13-15).

One serious family quarrel had dire consequences for the kingdom. Amnon, David's eldest son, lusted after his half-sister, Tamar. When Tamar resisted his advances, he lured her to his bedside, claiming to be ill. He then raped, and rejected her.

The king, learning of it, was angry but did nothing to Amnon since he particularly loved him as his firstborn. After two years, Tamar's full brother, Absalom, held a banquet at which he ordered his servants to kill Amnon. Absalom fled, remaining away for three years. Indicative of the problematic relationship between David and Joab, Joab connived to have David approve Absalom's return. David agreed, but would not see Absalom for two years (chapters 13 and 14).

Absalom, still angry at the king over Tamar, began to ingratiate himself by stationing himself at the entrance to Jerusalem, promising all who approached him that, if he were in charge, there would be full justice:

> "Thus Absalom did to every Israelite who came to the king for judgment; so Absalom stole the hearts of the people of Israel" (15.6).

After four years, Absalom went to Hebron, with the king's permission, where:

> "the conspiracy grew in strength, and the people with
> Absalom kept increasing" (15.12).

Absalom's power apparently caused David to flee on becoming convinced that conflict would have led to personal disaster.

One wonders about the loyalty that David enjoyed among the populace and the people's army. Only the mercenaries seem to have accompanied the fleeing king and his entourage (15.18).

In David's absence, Mephibosheth, whom David had protected, declared that his grandfather, Saul's, kingdom had been given to him (16.3).

That there remained pro-House of Saul individuals is testified to by Shimei's blast:

> "Out! Out! Murderer! Scoundrel! The Lord has avenged on all
> of you the blood of the house of Saul…" (16.7-8a).

Upon entering Jerusalem, Absalom was proclaimed king. His advisor, Ahithophel, counseled him to have public sex with David's concubines thereby affirming his power, and his position as his father's successor (16.15-23).

Ahithophel then advised Absalom to attack David with a large force, one which would encourage David's troops to desert, so the old king could then be easily killed.

Another advisor, who (unlike Ahithophel) was loyal to David, suggested that a standing-army force would be defeated and that to overwhelm David's army, Absalom should wait until he mobilized a much larger one from all of Israel. David and his men fled across the Jordan River. Ahithophel committed suicide; Absalom then appointed Amasa as his general - in place of Joab (chapter 17).

David's more experienced army soundly defeated Absalom's force. Whilst fleeing, Absalom's hair became entangled in a tree so that he hung there as his mule rode on.

Joab found him and, against David's orders, had his men kill him. Perhaps Joab was attempting to ingratiate himself with the king after having earlier alienated him. David's lament after learning of Absalom's death would indicate the contrary:

"O my son Absalom, my son, my son Absalom! Would that I
had died instead of you, O Absalom, my son, my son!"
(18.33b).

Joab's conflict with David is exhibited by his remonstrating with the king
after he had the usurper, Absalom, killed (19.1-8).

Shimei, who had cursed David as he fled, now appealed to David.
David did not punish him but later would advise Solomon to have him
killed (19.18-23).

Similarly, Mephibosheth pleaded with David, blaming his servant
for misguiding him in proclaiming himself king. David forgave him again
(19.24-30).

Antagonism between the north and south continued, with each side
claiming to be more loyal to David (19.41-43).

An Israelite rabble-rouser, Sheba, aroused the north against David:

"We have no portion in David, no share in the son of Jesse!
Everyone to your tents, O Israel!" (20.1).

The hostility between the regions would culminate in the split after the
reign of Solomon.

Meanwhile, David felt that Sheba was presenting a threat greater
than that of Absalom. He had Joab lead forces pursuing Sheba. With the
help of a woman in his refuge, Sheba was killed and his head thrown over
the city wall to Joab; that threat was ended (20.14-22).

As an aftermath, the royal administration was enlarged:

"Now Joab was in command of all the army of Israel; Benaiah
son of Jehoiada was in command of the Cherethites and the
Pelethites; Adoram was in charge of the forced labor;
Jehoshaphat son of Ahilud was the recorder; Sheva was
secretary; Zadok and Abiatar were priests; and Ira the Jairite
was also David's priest" (20.23-26).

Throughout all these conflicts, David still pursued any descendent of Saul
who might serve as rallying points for those opposing David. An example
inferred in DH indicating that a prolonged famine resulted from Saul's
mistreating the Gibeonites:

"Now there was a famine in the days of David for three years,
year after year; and David inquired of the Lord. The Lord said,
'There is blood-guilt on Saul and on his house, because he put

the Gibeonites to death.' So the king called the Gibeonites and
spoke to them. Now the Gibeonites were not of the people of
Israel, but of the remnant of the Amorites; although the people
of Israel had sworn to spare them, Saul had tried to wipe them
out in his zeal for the people of Israel and Judah." (21.1-2).
   Inquiring regarding what recompense they required, they demanded:
      "seven of his sons be handed over to them" (21.6).
David delivered the two sons of Saul's concubine, Rizpah, and the five
sons of Saul's daughter, Merab [the MT has her as Michal] (21.1-9).
      More successful battles were fought against the Philistines and the
Moabites (21.15-22; 23.8-39). Apparently, all these conflicts did not
permanently vanquish Israel's enemies.

David's end-of-life career and decisions are detailed in the first two
chapters of the first book of Kings.
      Believing that his father, David, was near death, his eldest son,
Adonijah, declared that he would be king. Now, there were two conflicting
royal groups.
      While Adonijah conferred with Joab and Aviatar, those in favor of
Solomon opposed Adonijah's nomination. These opponents included
Zadok, Benaiah, Nathan, Shimei and Rei. Rei and Shimei were probably
royal officers and Shimei is not he who cursed David.
      With Bathsheba's aid, David, recalling an early pledge he had
made to her, declared Solomon to be his successor.
      When Adonijah learned that Solomon had been anointed king, he
sought sanctuary at the altar.
   Solomon responded:
      "if he proves to be a worthy man, not one of his hairs shall fall
      to the ground; but if wickedness is found in him, he shall die.
      …He came to do obeisance to King Solomon; and Solomon
      said to him, 'Go home.'" (1 Kings 1.53; 1-52).

David's last charge begins with the DH formula "obey God and prosper,"
followed by secular, real-politik instructions: execute Joab who had
contended with him and who favored Adonijah and Shimei, the
Benjaminite, who cursed him and could not be trusted (2.1-9).
      Later Solomon would also find reason to execute Adonijah and
Aviatar, thus eliminating those who had opposed him or who could

continue to be threats. With this accomplished, the historian could conclude:

> "So the kingdom was established in the hand of Solomon" (2.46b; 9-46a).

The pro-Solomon group included Benaiah, the leader of the omnipresent mercenaries; a high priest, Zadok; Nathan, the king's advisor; and Bathsheba, the king's favorite wife. They were clearly more powerful and influential than those promoting Adonijah. This thoroughly secular account parallels other military and political movements: those backed by sufficient power and drive to overcome all opposition to their replacement of older forms.

A SECULAR ENCAPSULATION OF THE EARLY MONARCHY

David's drive for power was as the representative of Judah, the southern tribe. They were a clan whose lot lay in rough terrain, a country far less productive than the land of the northern tribes. While Israelite survival depended on being able to fend off neighbors (particularly Philistines) the ways this might be accomplished were open-ended.

Leaders of society opted for a dynastic monarchy, selecting Saul as a transitional king. Saul's own tribe did not have sufficient power, nor could his successor, Ishbaal, withstand the army of David.

The less developed south defeated, and then controlled the larger and more developed north that was unable to mobilize itself sufficiently to defeat David. This was not for lack of trying: it took David seven and a half years to be declared king of Israel, and this was only accomplished through conflict.

To consolidate his power, David systematically eliminated Saul's descendents and defeated insurgencies from within his own ranks and family. However, Israel never fully resolved the central issue: achieving full-unity so that it could remain independent. The unified kingdom lasted only through the reign of Solomon. After the north split off, its ten tribes continued to have dynastic difficulties until being conquered by Assyria in 722.

David's accomplishments were significant:.

- He created a standing professional army, which was effective against enemies within and without.

- With his census, he was able to develop a system for taxation and control.
- He developed a strong, independent capital in Jerusalem with a bureaucracy to manage the realm.
- With a joint high priesthood, he could further consolidate his power by using the mobilizing effect of the sacrificial cult.
- He overcame insurrections and was able to turn a functioning regime over to his son, Solomon.
- His mini-empire extended across the Jordan River and included Damascus to the north, Etzion-gever to the south, and the Arabian desert in the east.
- He checked the Philistines so that they were no longer a serious threat. He even incorporated many of them into his professional army.
- David's use of power demonstrates that he understood that power is the currency of politics.

Chapter Fifteen

*Wherein is enumerated many kings
from Solomon to Ahaziah and
Baasha of Israel and Judah,
emphasizing their poor adherence
to God which was to lead to the fall
of those kingdoms. First Kings lays
the groundwork for what was
readying itself to happen in 722 &
586.*

FIRST KINGS

The two books of Kings comprise a single unit. Its first part tells of Solomon's ascent, his reign, his building the Temple, and his royal palace in Jerusalem (1 Kings 1-11). Its second part tells of the splitting of the kingdom and the 722 conquest by Assyria of the northern kingdom: Israel (1 Kings 12-2 Kings 17). These books conclude with the conquest of Judaea by Babylonia in 586 (2 Kings 18-25).

While it contains considerable narration about the reigns of Solomon, Reheboam and Jereboam I, and the Elijah/Elisha cycle, Kings writes little of substance concerning the books' other central characters.

The essentially secular accounts found abundantly within Samuel are absent in Kings. The general framework for Kings is sacred. The secular nature of much that occurred during this period, however, may be extrapolated from the accounts offered. This overwhelmingly sacred account is based on secular records: the annals of Solomon; of the Kings of Israel, and the Kings of Judaea (1 Kings 11.41; 14.19; 14.20).

For the most part, this sacred history confirms that the kingdoms were conquered due to the misguided policies of monarchs who allowed, and often promoted, idolatry. This sacred history may be denoted as '*historic*': that is, non-factual (or ideological) history. It was framed to promote a specific goal: the idea that the kings (with only two exceptions: Hezekiah and Josiah) either allowed or enhanced idolatry. Therefore worshipping God had to be centralized in the Temple in Jerusalem in order to ensure the purity of exclusive loyalty to Yahweh (as well as the cultic expressions of this loyalty) and that God's rule could best be insured under the charge of his direct servants: the priests.

The last historians of Kings reflected the post-exilic reality. After the Persian conquest of Babylonia in 538, the Persians put priests in charge of Judaea. The DH held a special role in maintenance of the Davidic dynasty through repetition of a divine promise that the Davidic dynasty was to be eternal (2 Samuel 7.11), due to God's love for David (1 Kings 11.12; 2 Kings 8.19; 19.34). There was always the hope that a future monarchy would be restored, and the sacred text would be validated by God's role in its establishment.

The historic or sacred history held that idolatry was rampant throughout the Era of Kingdoms. Even with King Hezekiah's reforms, during the reign of his grandson, Josiah paganism was the norm. Kings does tell that King Josiah destroyed all expressions of idolatry and their practitioners (2 Kings 23).

Kings' judgment that most of the kings were evil promoters of idolatry, little diminished their regal effectiveness. Manasseh is a prototypical evil king, and he ruled for fifty-five years. Whatever his role in idolatry, he must have been quite an effective king to have ruled peacefully that long. Virtually every king, beginning with Solomon, was proclaimed to be leading the Israelites astray until God's judgment was brought upon them in 722, and again in 586.

To prevent his populace from going to the Temple in Jerusalem (thereby threatening their loyalty to him), Jereboam, selected by God to rule over Israel, was later condemned for establishing shrines on his southern and northern borders. Jereboam became the DH model for the other corrupt kings of the northern kingdom.

The DH view is that God was in charge of history and would punish those who were disloyal to him. His power was so great that he could summon Assyria, Babylonia and Persia to carry out his will in punishing his rebellious adherents. The power of God was also exhibited in the miracles of Elijah and Elisha, who were devotedly loyal to him.

Contrasting with this sacred history is the secular history, which may be clearly discerned within the sacred accounts. The unity, which David accomplished, defeating the forces of Saul and his successors through military means, lasted only through the reign of Solomon. The northern ten tribes continued to feel exploited by Judah and sought redress from Solomon's son, Reheboam, only to meet with rejection: they rebelled, separated, and formed an independent entity: Israel.

The ten tribes forming Israel were disparate is seen from the general instability of the new nation: during its two hundred year existence, eight of its twenty kings ruled for a year or less. Most of those brief rulers were assassinated, so dynastic changes were frequent.

Rivalry between north and south resulted in their losing much of David's mini-empire. On occasion, Israel and Judaea did join together. More frequently, they allied themselves to foreign elements against each other. There were also periodic alliances with Egypt against the Mesopotamian empires: those attempts never met with success.

While the secularity of the societies is apparent in Kings, this secularity is more deeply embedded here than it was in Samuel. The DH increasingly realized that the survival of Judaea and Yahweh's adherents depended on emphasizing the religious aspects of their society, while downgrading secular elements, including their monarchies.

To insure Judaea's survival, Kings' history was presented in a way that furthered this goal. God was still present in history, and his people would survive if they maintained their exclusive loyalty to him. This historical approach, this sacred history, reinforced the ideology of Jeremiah and Isaiah of the Exile and proved successful. Those Israelites, who were exiled by Assyria in 722, lacking this history and ideology, were absorbed into Assyrian culture, while those exiled in 586 survived.

Throughout Kings, **the sacred** predominates!

Because Solomon is David's successor, he is glorified, but as king, he set the pattern for virtually all the kings that follow, until Judaea is conquered by Babylonia. DH has virtually all its kings committing idolatry, exhibiting serious disloyalty toward God and deserving of punishment. With few exceptions, little is related concerning those kings' careers. Far more is written about Solomon than any of the others.

SOLOMON

Once Solomon's kingdom is established, his first act is to form an alliance with Pharaoh by marrying one of his daughters (1 Kings 3.1). Then contrary to specific instructions from God against such marriages, he subsequently marries many more foreign wives:

"for they will surely incline your heart to follow their gods.
Solomon clung to these in love...For when Solomon was old,
his wives turned away his heart after other gods; and his heart
was not true to the Lord his God..." (11.2-4)

The secular account has Solomon marrying many foreign women. The
sacred account has him setting a bad precedent for his successors, leading
to the dissolution of his unified kingdom. Though this occurred for general
economic and political reasons, DH consistently blame it on disobedience
toward God, particularly his commandment not to worship other gods.

Sacred accounts include elements of the:
- o   construction of the Temple in Jerusalem;
- o   details of its décor and accoutrements;
- o   transfer of the Ark of the Covenant to the Temple;
- o   its dedication;
- o   the sacrifices offered on that occasion.

DH typically exaggerates numbers of troops, wives and sacrifices.
    Solomon is said to have 700 wives and 300 concubines (11.3);
    In its dedication, 22,000 oxen & 120,000 sheep were sacrificed
(8.63; Ch 6,7,8).

Secular accounts feature Solomon's wisdom. The best-known example is
the story of the two women who came before him, each claiming that a
particular child was hers. Through Solomon's wisdom, the woman who
was willing to spare the child was known to be the true mother. Then:

"all Israel heard the judgment that the king had rendered; and
they stood in awe of the king, because they perceived that the
wisdom of God was in him to execute justice" (3.28; 16-27).

Several other similar statements reinforce this attribute:

"God gave Solomon very great wisdom, discernment, and
breadth of understanding as vast as the sand on the seashore,
so that Solomon's wisdom surpassed the wisdom of all the
people of the east, and all the wisdom of Egypt...People came
from all the nations to hear the wisdom of Solomon; they
came from all the kings of the earth who had heard of his
wisdom" (4.29-34).

This was part of the glorification of Solomon by DH for his role in
building the Temple.

Solomon established a bureaucracy to govern his empire, the extent of which was also exaggerated to span: from the Euphrates to the land of the Philistines, even to the border of Egypt. In this account, he had 40,000 stalls of horses for his chariots and 12,000 horsemen (Ch. 4).

Besides building the Temple, which took seven years, with the help of Hiram, king of Tyre, he built his palace in thirteen years. That Tyre was tributary to Israel is noted by his being compensated for timber and gold with twenty cities in Galilee, a compensation Hiram considered inadequate (9.10-14).

The dimensions of the Temple were far smaller than those of the palace, which possessed more than four times its volume, indicating that the secular realm dominated the sacred. Moreover, the detail and wealth invested in the palace far exceeded that of the Temple (chapter seven).

Solomon used forced labor from conquered peoples to help build palace and Temple and other buildings, as well as his fortress cities: Hazor, Meggido and Gezer. That Israel was not as technologically as advanced as some of its neighbors is evidenced by the use of skilled craftsmen and naval sailors from Tyre (chapter 9).

The episode with the Queen of Sheba, who visited Solomon, is indicative of his international trade with her and others. His wealth is summarized by:

"Thus King Solomon excelled all the kings of the earth in riches..." (10.23; 10.1-29).

While Solomon may have indeed been an effective king, the secular material about him is greatly exaggerated. That his empire was not as vast and secure as the text implies is clear from conflicts with Aram and Edom. As is usual in Kings, whenever anything goes against the monarch, it is God's doing:

"Then the Lord raised up an adversary against Solomon, Hadad the Edomite...Rezon, the king of Aram....was an adversary of Israel all the days of Solomon..." (11.14, 23).

Occasionally, Solomon's glorification is apparently intruded upon by historical reality. Internal discontent did exist although little of it is detailed.

Jereboam, an Ephraimite, was Solomon's officer in charge of forced labor. He must have displeased Solomon in some way, since he fled to Egypt. Later Jereboam would return to lead the ten northern tribes out of the unified state. Deuteronomic historians, maintaining the sacred orientation of history, have God select him to do this (11.26-40).

A SUCCESSION OF KINGS

With Solomon's death, his son, Reheboam, ascended his throne. Indicative of the discontent in the north, Jereboam, apparently beckoned by his fellow-Ephraimites, returned from Egypt. He then led a delegation to the new king to seek a lessening of taxes and demands that Solomon had imposed on them. He had exploited the ten northern tribes, which had been conquered by David and then held subservient. They now sought redress. This secular account makes perfect sense.

Reheboam consulted with his older, and younger colleagues. The older advised to lighten the burdens; the younger advised making them heavier. The older men were established and sought to maintain what they had, even if in the future there would be less for them. The younger men understood that for them to gain what the others had more would be required of their subjects, particularly since the north's population was far greater. When their appeal was rejected, the north broke away and, with rare exceptions, the relationship between the regimes of those two regions was hostile.

Jereboam was made king over Israel. In the sacred account Deuteronomic historians, of course, attributed this to the Lord fulfilling his words, that as a consequence of Solomon's apostasy, his kingdom would be split (12.1-25).

Recognizing the importance of the Temple in Jerusalem as a unifying force for the monarchy in Judaea, Jereboam established cult centers in Bethel, just north of Jerusalem, and in Dan near the northern border of Israel. He introduced the worship of bulls in these centers, utilizing non-Levites for his shrines (12.25-33).

Just as a prophet had predicted to Jereboam that Solomon's kingdom would be split and most of it given to him, now 'a man of God' predicted that his altars would be destroyed unless he changed his ways. DH's sacred account then has judgment called down upon Jereboam:

> "Even after this event, Jereboam did not turn from his evil way, but made the priests of the high places[3] again from among all the people; any who wanted to be priests he consecrated for the high places. This matter became a sin to the house of Jereboam, so as to cut it off and to destroy it from the face of the earth" (13.33-34; 1-32).

Idolatry not only pervaded Israel: Reheboam's Judaea, was no better. Under him, Judaea "provoked God…with their sins, more than all that their ancestors had done" (14.22-24).

That was a litany following most kings in both nations. DH certainly knew that, for the most part, the kings, by leading their people to sin were evil, and had to be replaced.

- Early in Reheboam's reign, Pharaoh Shishak invaded Judaea and removed to Egypt all treasures in Jerusalem's palace and Temple (14.25-28).
- As was the case until the conquest of Israel, constant war raged between north and south (14.30; 15.6, 16, 32).
- Asa and Jehoshaphat joining together against Aram was a rare exception.
- Abijah succeeded Reheboam and served for three years. He also is described as a sinner, committing the same sin as his father (15.1-8).
- His son, Asa, ruled for forty-one years. Perhaps in recognition of his successful longevity, he was described as doing "what was right in the sight of the Lord," destroying idols but allowing the high places to remain (15.9-15).

Deuteronomic historians would repeat this mantra over most of the kings. Only with Hezekiah and Josiah would the high places be destroyed, being permanently eliminated only by Josiah. That brought about DHs' goal: exclusive consolidation of the cult within Jerusalem.

The war between Israel and Judaea was prolonged:

- Asa went to Ben Hadad, king of Aram, to pay him to break his alliance with Israel. Ben Hadad agreed, conquering some of

---

[3] Cultic structures on hills and mountains: e.g., those at Ramah, Shechem, Bethel, Gilgal, and Shiloh.

Israel's territory, and Judaea gaining some of the war spoils (15.16-24).

- Nadab, son of Jereboam, reigned for only two years, possibly because he also did what was evil in the sight of the Lord (15.25-26). Nadab's death was symptomatic of the political instability of Israel.
- While besieging a Philistine city, an officer, Baasha, killed Nadab and succeeded him as king. He also killed all of Jereboam's descendants, fulfilling God's promise to wipe out the house of Jereboam because of his sins (15.27-30).

There was no effective unity between north and south, other than that which was forced. This was also true of the tribal components of the north. The ten tribes never fully coalesced into a securely bound nation.

- o Because Baasha also did evil, God, through a prophet, indicated that he would wipe out all of Baasha's descendents.
- o This took place after his son, Elah, had been king for two years. One of his commanders, Zimri, killed Elah while he was drunk, and then proceeded to kill all of his family and friends.
- o Zimri did not last very long either – seven days: the shortest reign of any of the kings. A rebellion against him led by Omri had him trapped, leading him to commit suicide.
- o Instability continued as Israel split between Omri and Tibni, with Omri killing Tibni, becoming king.
- o He, too, "did what was evil," and died after seven years (16.1-28).

The DH offer very little information, if any, about the general conditions of the nations. Their only interest is to indicate how evil the kings' actions were to causatively explain the conquest of Israel - and later Judaea – as proof that God was the author of history.

Omri's son, Ahab, who married Jezebel, the daughter of the king of Sidon was, of course, the most evil of all. Jezebel, through Ahab, may be the one who formally introduced -- or reintroduced -- and emphasized the worship of Baal (16.28-34).

It is at this point that Elijah is introduced. Elijah was the leader of a guild of prophets portrayed as Yahweh exclusivists. He and his successor, Elisha, are featured in Kings' next sixteen chapters. Indicative of Elijah's loyalty to God was his power to perform miracles, primarily healing and food miracles.

The principle purpose of the narratives about kings was to dramatize the reality and power of God through prophetic words and actions. These narratives reinforced the sacred nature of Kings. It related very little history other than:

- ❖ names of those kings;
- ❖ lengths of their reigns;
- ❖ how they led their people astray;
- ❖ and how they were punished.

When King Ben Hadad of Aram attacked Israel, Ahab was successful. To frame this secular event, DH has God predicting his victory via an unnamed prophet.

This process is repeated in a subsequent battle when Ben Hadad restores territory he had conquered, and agrees to be tributary to Israel (20.13, 19-34).

A story, reminiscent of the David-Bathsheba-Uriah episode, concerns Ahab's desire to confiscate the vineyard of Naboth. When Naboth refuses to give it up, Ahab has him killed. Elijah, speaking for God, tells Ahab that he too, will be killed. Perhaps to conform to history, it is told that, when Ahab humbles himself before Elijah's condemnation and threat, God has Elijah say that while Ahab will not then be killed, disaster would come during his son's lifetime (21.1-29).

Israel and Judaea rarely fought as allies, but they did when Jehoshaphat went to Ahab to suggest that they join together against Aram. During the ensuing battle, Ahab was killed (22.1-4, 29-40).

Jehoshaphat was accounted "right in the sight of the Lord" but he too, failed to remove the high places where citizens continued to sacrifice. Ahaziah, Ahab's son, ruled for just two years. His premature death was presumably due to his worship of Baal thereby provoking God (22.43, 51-53).

Chapter Sixteen

*The fracturing of David's mini-
empire continues as two kingdoms
of one people bicker about where
sacrifices to YHWH may be made.
Assyria and Babylon settle the
matter by destroying all sacrificial
centers and exiling the people.*

SECOND KINGS

The second book of Kings includes two watershed events, events that
proved crucial for the future of the Jewish people.

✓ **(1)** The dramatic conquest of the ten northern tribes (Israel), with
exile of most of their populations. These so-called *lost ten tribes*
were in reality lost only in the sense that they lost their special
identity, on being absorbed into Assyrian culture.

✓ **(2)** This motivated some sensitive individuals in the two
remaining tribes of Judaea to do what they could to prevent such a
fate for them should they experience a similar conquest. These
individuals - ideologues known as prophets – invented an approach
to history and the future in order to insure their people's survival.
136 years after Israel fell, Babylonia conquered Judaea and exiled
most of its population into Babylon.

Preeminent among these prophets were Jeremiah and Isaiah of the Exile.
Also included are the Deuteronomic historians who structured the history
of Israel in such a way that God was in control of history and aligned with
them.

While one may detect secular history in 2-Kings, it overwhelmingly
focuses on:

- God determines events;
- Judaeans would continue as long as their faith in God continued;
- and they adhered to his demands.

With Babylon's conquest of Judaea, this approach would be tested. The
fact that those exiled maintained their identity in exile, as well as when
some returned to Judaea, proved its effectiveness.

Most kings being discussed are described as evil promoters of idolatry. Even when a long-reigning king seems to have been effective, he generally permitted those high places to exist; on this account, he was counted among the evil kings. Kings who moved against idolatry, nevertheless, allowed the high places to continue sacrificing. The assumption was that the worship of Yahweh, taking place there, was less-than-pure. This would be the reason given for the Josianic command to destroy all of the high places: allowing the cult to be observed only in the Temple in Jerusalem. Whenever any king had success, his triumphs were inevitably attributed to Yahweh's importance.

Deuteronomy (12.2) describes 'high places' as being: "on the high mountains and upon the hills and under every green tree." 2Kings 17.9 places some in towns; Jer 7.31; 32.35 and Ezel 6.3 mention valleys. The high places (*bemot*; sg. *bema*) were a common cultic feature in nations surrounding Israel; they typically were described as places where idolatrous rites were practiced. Centralizing the worship of Yahweh required their destruction. Prior to this, the highly regarded priest/prophet, Samuel, offered sacrifices at the high place of Ramah (1 Sam 10.5).

ISRAEL

In the secular realm, it is clear from the text that neither Israel, nor Judaea, could long control David's ancient mini-empire. While occasionally a regional enemy would be reconquered, the trend was toward a steadily shrinking territory. Moab, Edom and especially Aram (Damascus) proved troublesome.

In time, the major empires in the northeast, Assyria and Babylonia, would each defeat a Jewish kingdom, and exile its population. From time to time, Israel and Judaea would politically turn to their large neighbor, the once-all-powerful Egypt. However, any assistance coming from that quarter proved temporary, if not ineffective.

With the siege of Jerusalem, the conquest of Judaea and the destruction of the Temple, survival of the people rested on ideology and will, rather than any material or physical assets.

A single sentence in Kings mentions that:
- Moab rebelled after the death of Ahab;
- Ahab's son, Ahaziah, had an accident;

- Ahajiah sent messengers to inquire of Baal-zebub, the god of Ekron in Phoenicia.

God, incensed at this disloyalty, had Elijah advise Ahaziah that he was to die. The king sent several bands of fifty men to appeal to Elijah, who had God destroy them by fire. God would not be placated: the king died (2 Kings 1.1-18).

The next king of Israel was Jehoram, another son of Ahab: he reigned for twelve years. He was, we are informed, evil (3.1-3).

While Jehoram was Israel's king, King Mesha of Moab rebelled against Israel. Jehoram called upon King Jehoshaphat of Judaea to join his battle against Moab. This was one of very few occasions when the two adjoining states cooperated (3. 4-8)

The remainder of this episode is in the sacred mode: God provided water during a drought and promised success against Moab. Elisha, assuring the King of Israel of this states:

"This is only a trifle in the sight of the Lord, for he will hand
Moab over to you" (3. 9-27).

God acts similarly during a war with Aram. He strikes them blind and the siege of Samaria is lifted by divine intervention (6.8-7.20).

Having married the daughter of Ahab, Joram (Jehoram), the son of Jehoshaphat, was also accounted evil. This marriage may have been done to cement the alliance between Israel and Judaea against Moab. Although the king was evil:

"Yet the Lord would not destroy Judaea, for the sake of David,
since he promised to give a lamp to him and his descendants
forever" (8.16-19).

This verse may have been placed here to perpetuate the special role of David, and provide a basis for his restored monarchy should that happen after 586. A weakening of Judaea's territorial integrity is implied by rebellions in both Edom and Libnah (8.20-22). The alliance between the north and south continued as Jehoram, the son of Ahab in his war against King Hazael of Aram was joined by Ahaziah, son of King Jehoram of Judaea (8.26-29).

A sacred and a secular account follow one another in Jehu's overthrowing Ahab's dynasty. In the sacred account: a member of Elisha's prophetic group is sent to Jehu, a commander of the military, conveying a message from God:

❖ "I anoint you king over the people of the Lord, over Israel. You shall strike down the house of your master Ahab... for the whole house of Ahab shall perish; I will cut off from Ahab every male, bond or free, in Israel..." (9.1-13).

❖ In the secular account,

- Jehu attacks both Jehoram and Ahaziah as they were assembled against Aram and kills them (9.14-37).

- He then proceeds to kill not only the entire house of Ahab but also their leaders, close friends and priests (10. 11, 17).

- While Jehu did well for God, wiping out Baal worship, he generally remained a sinner, maintaining idolatrous shrines in Dan and Bethel (10.28-31).

Aram's success over Israel also came from God:

"In those days the Lord began to trim off parts of Israel. Hazael defeated them throughout the territory of Israel" (10.32-33).

Dynastic disputes continued.

When Ahaziah was killed by Jehu, his mother, Athaliah, sought to destroy the royal family. Ahaziah's sister saved one of his sons, Joash, by hiding him for six years. Subsequently, the priest Jehoiada led a revolt. Jehoiada had Joash proclaimed king, and Athaliah was executed (11.1-21).

Joash, who began his reign at seven, ruled for forty years and while he was accounted good, the high places remained (12.1-3).

Once again Aram went on the march. It was bought off in Jerusalem (12.17-18).

The political situation being unsettled, Joash was killed by his servants (12.20).

Aram, constantly engaged in conflicts with mixed success, continued to trouble Israel. When Aram won, Deuteronomic historians had God in charge, and when Israel was saved, it was also God's doing:

"The anger of the Lord was kindled against Israel so that he gave them into the hand of King Hazael of Aram, then into the hand of Ben-hadad, son of Hazael...Therefore the Lord gave

Israel a savior, so that they escaped from the hand of the
Arameans..." (13.1-9; 22-25).
Relations between Israel and Judaea must have deteriorated as Joash
fought against Amaziah of Judah (13.12).

King Amaziah of Judaea had success against Edom (14.7). Because of this
success, he challenged Jehoash of Israel who attempted to defuse any
conflict.

When Amaziah persisted, he was captured. Jehoash broke down
much of the wall of Jerusalem, seizing all of the gold, silver, and vessels
from the Temple and the king's palace (14.8-14).

A conspiracy led to Amaziah's being killed with his son Azariah
proclaimed king (14.17-22).

Jereboam II succeeded his father Joash and restored much lost
territory of Israel. Though he was accounted evil by DH, he must have
been not only a very successful military leader, but also an effective
politician, since he ruled for forty-one years (14.23-29).

Azariah (Uzziah) was another effective king, reigning for fifty-two
years. But, while he did what was right in the sight of the Lord, people still
sacrificed in the high places (15.1-7).

Instability once again enveloped Israel:

Zechariah, the son of Jereboam, ruled for six months before being
assassinated in public by Shallum,

Shallum ruled for one month before being killed in his turn by
Menachem (15.8-16).

Menachem's reign began with Israel becoming an Assyrian vassal.
When confronted by the army of Tiglath-Pileser III, he paid a thousand
talents of silver as tribute (15.17-20).

Menachem's son, Pekahiah, had ruled for two years when his
captain, Pekah, killed him and occupied the throne (15.23-26).

Tiglath-Pileser returned, conquering much territory while carrying
away captives (15.29).

After ruling for twenty years, Pekah the assassin was assassinated
by Hoshea (15.30). Pekah had joined in an alliance with King Rezin of
Aram against Judah (15.37).

Rezin and Pekah had besieged Jerusalem, but could not conquer it (16.5). Edom, by conquering Elath, also proved successful against Judaea (16.6).

Alliances shifted constantly. King Ahaz of Judaea swore fealty to the Assyrians and requested their help against Israel and Aram. He also sent them a large tribute. Assyria then marched against Damascus and took it, killing King Rezin of Aram, and taking captives (16. 7-9).

During the reign of Hoshea, King Shalmaneser of Assyria continued holding Israel as it vassal. When Hoshea quit paying tribute, and approached Egypt for aid, Shalmaneser imprisoned him. Assyria then besieged Samaria for three years before taking it, and exiling most of its people (17.5-6; 18.9-12).

In the sacred account, this catastrophe came from God because of the people's sins, particularly the sin of worshipping other gods (17.7-23).

Assyria then transported non-Jewish foreigners to Israel. As a matter of course, they brought their own idolatrous cults to the northern land (17.24-41).

JUDAea [Judaea refers to the southern kingdom; Judah refers to its tribe]

Hezekiah, the son of Hoshea, was accounted as Judaea's best king ever:

"He trusted in the Lord the God of Israel; so that there was no one like him among all the kings of Judaea after him, or among those who were before him" (18.5). This was another DH exaggeration.

What does this tell us about David and Hezekiah's grandson, Josiah, of whom Deuteronomic historians denote as the best of reformers?

Hezekiah destroyed the idolatrous infrastructure of worshipping other gods.

- He must have felt powerful and protected;
- he rebelled against Assyria;
- stopped paying tribute;
- and successfully attacked the Philistines (18.7-8).
- When Assyria invaded Judaea and captured its fortified cities, Hezekiah again paid a very high tribute, three hundred talents of silver and thirty of gold.
- He apparently approached Egypt for assistance without success (18.13-16; 21-24).

The sacred account of the lifting of Assyria's siege of Jerusalem is credited to God:

> "That very night the angel of the Lord set out and struck down one hundred eighty-five thousand in the camp of the Assyrians; when morning dawned, they were all dead bodies. Then King Sennacharib of Assyria left and went home" (19.35-36; 5-7; 32-34).

Another, secular explanation may be that the king learned of problems in his capital, Nineveh. When he returned home, he was assassinated by two of his sons (19.37).

Hezekiah, who was succeeded by his son, Manasseh, was accounted so evil that God decided to destroy Jerusalem and allow the conquest of Judaea. Manasseh restored the idolatry his father had eliminated. He even sacrificed one of his sons; his general behavior was worse than that of any king before him. Yet he ruled for fifty-five years. In a secular sense, he must be accounted an effective ruler (21.1-18).

A far different view of Manasseh is given in the Book of Chronicles. Members of 'the priestly party' compiled this book approximately two hundred years after Kings. In that account, Manasseh is captured and taken to Assyria. There he prays and pleads with God, who allows him to be returned to Jerusalem, where he regains his crown. He also destroys idolatry and commands the people to serve God (2 Chronicles 33.10-17).

Just why a group exclusively loyal to Yahweh and the Temple cult would present a view of Manasseh so contrary to the judgment in Kings is not clear. Perhaps the lesson was that even someone as evil as Manasseh could repent and serve as a model for others. His son, Amon, is described to be as evil as his father. He was assassinated by some of his servants whom in turn, were themselves executed (21. 19-29).

Amon's son, Josiah, was viewed as exemplary. He had the Temple repaired. In the process, the high priest, Hilkiah, found 'the book of the law,' presumably a copy of the book of Deuteronomy or what was the basis for it:

> "He did what was right in the sight of the Lord, and walked in all the way of his father David; he did not turn aside to the right or to the left" (22.1-2).

Josiah, alone of all of the kings, actually eliminated idolatry. In particular, he had all of the high places destroyed. From his time on worship would be performed only in the Temple in Jerusalem, thereby consolidating the power of the Jerusalem priesthood and providing greater support for the king (22.3-22.24).

That Josiah was accounted the best of the kings is clear:

> "Before him there was no king like him, who turned to the Lord with all his heart, and with all his soul, and with all his might, according to all the Law of Moses; nor did any like him arise after him" (23.25).

The sacred account, however, did not conform to historical reality:

> Judaea was not spared conquest by Babylonia, even with Josiah's righteousness. Manasseh's sins were simply too great to be overcome (22.26-27).

> In an addendum, Josiah is described as challenging Pharaoh Necho, who was on his way to join Assyria so as to challenge an emerging Babylonia. When they met at Megiddo, Josiah was killed (23.29-30).

Just as the Chronicler rehabilitated Manasseh, he does the opposite with Josiah. In the Chronicles account, the Pharaoh tells Josiah that he has no conflict with him and that he, Necho, is following the will of God:

> "I am not coming against you today, but against the house with which I am at war; and God has commanded me to hurry. Cease opposing God, who is with me, so that he will not destroy you. But Josiah would not turn away…"(2 Chronicles 35.20-24).

Here we have two dramatically different sacred historical accounts, with the latter more in apparent conformity with what really happened. Josiah was a less effective ruler than his grandfather. DH preferred him while the Chronicler had him disobeying God. It is possible that Josiah's action against Necho was a pro-Assyrian act, leading to Judaea's conquest by an emerging Babylonia some twenty-five years later.

Josiah's son, Jehoahaz, had reigned for three months before being imprisoned by Pharaoh Necho. Necho made his brother, Eliakim (Jehoiakim) king, and extracted a large tribute for Egypt (23.31-37).

In 605, the Babylonians defeated the combined Egyptian and Assyrian armies at Carchemish; King Nebuchadnezar of Babylonia made Judaea a tributary.

- o   When Jehoiakim rebelled, God had all of Judah's neighbors attacking (24.1-7).
- o   under the overwhelming power of Babylonia, Egypt was no longer a factor, (24.7).
- o   Jehoiakim's son, Jehoiachin, gave himself up to the besieging Babylonians.
- o   They took the treasures of Jerusalem, their officials, all men who were fit for war, and skilled craftsmen, as captives.

The Babylonians then made Jehoiachin's uncle, Zedekiah, king.

When he rebelled, Nebuchadnezzar again besieged Jerusalem. On capturing Zedekiah, they killed his sons, blinded him, and hauled him off to Babylon. They then destroyed the Temple and all major buildings of Jerusalem and took most of the remainder of the population into exile, leaving only the poorest of the land (24.17-25.12).

Chaos regulated the Jerusalem community. The king of Babylonia had appointed Gedaliah to govern those remaining in Judah. After governing for seven months, he was assassinated. The assassins and those allied with them fled to Egypt (25.22-26; Jeremiah 40.13-41.18).

Nothing else is known of events in Judah until the return of some from exile following Persia's conquest of Babylonia in 538.

AFTEr THE EXiLES RETURN

The rebuilding job of Jerusalem and Judah is reported in the books of Nehemiah and Ezra. These books cover the period around 450. Nehemiah rebuilt the walls and other infrastructures; Ezra represented those who finalized the Torah, which became the governing law of a society that now was thoroughly sacralized.

Secular history had no place in this new Judaean environment. Judaeans had little military power or political independence (Nehemiah; Ezra).

Persians delegated power to the priesthood, which they saw as no threat to their imperial control. The raison d'être of Judaean society was to be its sacrificial cult centered in the rebuilt Temple in Jerusalem, and the gradually developing Judaism with a full-blown ideology that its prophets initially had developed.

Chapter Seventeen

A fast excursion through Prophets:
the good [true], the bad [false],
and the unlikely.

THE PROPHETS: AN INTRODUCTION

When it comes to important figures in the Hebrew Bible, THE PROPHETS form a major category.

The literal translation of the Hebrew word for prophet is ***navee*** (plural: ***n'vee-eem***), meaning 'to call or speak forth.' The prophet is one who is a spokesman for God. Other, synonymous Hebrew words are ***chozeh***, one who sees visions, and ***roe-eh***, a seer. Samuel, the priest/prophet/judge, is called both roe-eh (1 Samuel 9.9) and navee (1 Samuel 3.20). According to 1 Samuel 9.9, the use of roe-eh anteceded that of navee.

Several individuals in the Hebrew Bible are called prophets, but little of their prophetic career is noted. Of Abraham, we read:

"For he is a prophet and he will pray for you and you shall live" (addressed to King Abimelech; Genesis 20.7).

Moses is denoted as being above all other prophets: while God communicated to other prophets through visions, only to Moses did he speak face to face (Numbers 12.6f.). His brother, Aaron, is also called a prophet, although his major role was that of priest (Exodus 7.1). Their sister, Miriam, is similarly denoted as a prophetess (Exodus 15.20).

Many prophets were involved with kings, serving as intermediaries between the human kings and the supreme sovereign, God. Nathan was the prophet to King David, revealing God's will to him, but also serving as a court advisor in political affairs. He delivered an oracle from God to David (2 Samuel 7.1-17); that indicated divine disapproval concerning David's adulterous affair with Bathsheba, which had led to David having her husband killed in battle (2 Samuel 12.1-14); Nathan later included Bathsheba and the commander of the Standing Army, Benaiah, to have David appoint Solomon as his successor, instead of Adonijah, his older son (1Kings 22.29-39.)

After the death of Solomon, Ahijah indicated to Jereboam that God had selected Jereboam to lead the ten northern tribes (1Kings 11.29-39).

Elijah and Elisha led a group of prophets during the Omiride regime as described in 1-Kings 17-2 Kings 10. Many legends about them are in these chapters, including miraculous food and healing miracles. They were Yahweh exclusivists and they fought monarchs who were just as happy favoring Baal and Asherah.

There were foreign prophets; Jezebel entertained 450 prophets of Baal and 400 prophets of Asherah. After the contest between Yahweh and Baal resulted in a decisive victory for Yahweh, Elijah had the foreign prophets killed (1 Kings 18.19, 40).

Another foreign prophet, one who favored Yahweh was Balaam, a native of Pethor on the Euphrates. Balak the king of Moab, fearful of the Israelites after their defeat of Ammon, sought to hire Balaam to curse Israel. His response was no doubt unsatisfactory:

"I have come to you now, but do I have power to say anything? The word God puts in my mouth, that is what I must say" (Numbers 22.38).

Another type of prophets were the Ecstatics. Samuel described them to Saul thusly:

"...as you come to the town, you will meet a band of prophets coming down from the shrine with harp, tambourine, flute and lyre playing in front of them; they will be in a prophetic frenzy. Then the spirit of the Lord will possess you and you will be in a prophetic frenzy along with them and turned into a different person" (1 Samuel 10.5f.).

As noted, there were professional prophets who would tell those who paid them what they wished to hear. Jeremiah condemned this group:

"For the least to the greatest of them, everyone is greedy for unjust gain; from the prophet to priest, everyone deals falsely. They have treated the wound of my people carelessly, saying, 'Peace, peace,' when there is no peace" (Jeremiah 6.13f.).

And Jeremiah warned King Zedekiah:

"Do not listen to the words of the prophets who are telling you not to serve the King of Babylon, for they are prophesying a lie to you. I have not sent them, says the Lord, but they are prophesying falsely in my name..." (27.14f.).

PRE-EXILIC PROPHETS

AMOS

Just as there were different kinds of prophets, the prophets themselves came from a variety of class backgrounds.

Amos, possibly the first of these prophets, was of the rural working class. He is presented as a Judaean shepherd who also trimmed sycamore trees in Tekoa. He acknowledges that he is neither a prophet nor the son of a prophet, yet he proclaims :
"The Lord said to me, 'Go, prophesy to my people Israel" (1.1; 7.14f.).
Amos's prophecy comes about 750, during the long (786-746) and peaceful reign of Israel's King Jereboam II. During his reign, Israel reached its greatest prosperity and territorial extent, a peak never attained again. Society's leaders considered this a sign of God's special favor, and so he continued to support official shrines.

Amos, in (presumably) a single exhortation, denied their erroneous assumptions, asserting instead the regime's reliance on the military and empty rituals was vain. He further forcefully pointed out that social injustice, and personal immorality, would lead to doom. Within forty years, his prophecy came true. Assyria conquered Israel and exiled most of its population.

A hallmark of Amos' prophecy was his clear declaration that there is a single, all-powerful God for all of humanity. At this time, the Israelites were monolatrous; they worshipped their god as special while acknowledging the reality of other deities. As the last chapters of 2-Kings and the Josianic reforms testify, some Israelites continued to worship so until 586 when the first Temple was destroyed. Amos may have been the first monotheist, but it would take over 200 years more for Israelite society to accept this *'reality.'*

In the first two chapters, Amos notes that God is not only in control of the fate of Judaea and Israel, but of other nations as well: Aram (Damascus), Gaza, Edom, Ashdod, Ekron, Tyre, Ammon, and Moab. This is summarized in this statement:

"'Are you, not like the Cushites (Ethiopians) to me, O house of Israel?' says the Lord. 'Did I not bring Israel up from the land of Egypt, and the Philistines from Caphtor and the Arameans from Kir?'" (Amos 9.7).

This universalism did not replace the idea of Israel being chosen by God. It simply underlines its greater responsibility:

"You only have I known of all the families of the earth; therefore I will punish you for all your iniquities" (3.2).

While the sacred -- the role and power of God -- pervades Amos' prophecies, the values he evokes are completely secular. Indeed, the sacred as expressed in the cult and rituals is clearly devalued. While Amos and those who preserved his prophecies operated in the sacred mode, what they stated was in effect secular.

> "Thus says the Lord: For three transgressions of Israel, and for four, I will not revoke the punishment; because they sell the righteous for silver, and the needy for a pair of sandals -- they who trample the head of the poor into the dust of the earth, and push the afflicted out of the way..." (2.6f.).

> "I will tear down their winter house as well as the summer house; and the houses of ivory shall perish, and the great houses shall come to an end" (3.15).

> "Seek good and not evil, that you may live; and so the Lord, the God of hosts, will be with you, just as you have said. Hate evil and love good, and establish justice within the gate; it may be that the Lord the God of hosts, will be gracious to the remnant of Joseph" (5.14f.).

There is no stronger statement in the Hebrew Bible against the cult, its rituals, and sacrifices than when Amos gives the message from God in the most forcible terms possible.

"I hate, I despise your festivals, and I take no delight in your solemn assemblies. Even though you offer me your burnt offerings and grain offerings, I will not accept them; and the offerings of well-being of your fatted animals I will not look upon. Take away from me the noise of your songs; I will not listen to the melody of your harps. But let justice roll down as waters, and righteousness like an ever-flowing stream" (5.21-24).

Amos even denies that there were sacrifices during the Exodus:
"Did you bring me sacrifices and offerings the forty years in the wilderness, O house of Israel?" (5.25).

The judgment on Israel for their sins was to be swift and complete:

- ❖ "So I will send fire on Judah, and it shall devour the strongholds of Jerusalem" (2.5).

- ❖ "Alas for you who desire the day of the Lord! Why do you want the day of the Lord? It is darkness, not light; as if someone fled from a lion, and was met by a bear; or went into the house and rested a hand against the wall, and was bitten by a snake. Is not the day of the Lord darkness, not light, and gloom with no brightness in it?" (5.18-20).

- ❖ "You shall take up Sakkuth your king and Kaiwan your star-god (Assyrian gods), your images which you made for yourselves; therefore I will take you into exile beyond Damascus, says the Lord, whose name is God of hosts" (5.26f.).

- ❖ "The eyes of the Lord God are upon the sinful kingdom, and I will destroy it from the face of the earth -- except I will not utterly destroy the house of Jacob, says the Lord. For lo, I will command and shake the house of Israel among the nations as one shakes with a sieve, but no pebble shall fall to the ground. All the sinners of my people shall die by the sword, who say 'Evil shall not overtake or meet us'"(9.8-10).

ISAIAH

Scholars have long noted that this book contains prophecies of many different ideologies spanning a 300-year interval. It began before Assyria's conquest of Israel through the 586 conquest of Judaea, including the return of many Judaeans after Cyrus of Persia's conquest of the Middle East.

The first Isaiah, also called Isaiah of Jerusalem, seems to have been a court official and may have been of a priestly family. Much of the first 39 chapters are attributed to him. Some scholars call the author of 40-55 'Isaiah of the Exile' (or Deutero-Isaiah); this Isaiah responded to the conquest of Judaea by Babylon and its Babylonian exile of most citizens. Chapters 56-66 are attributed to anonymous poets collectively called Trito-Isaiah. They too were post-exilic.

Isaiah of Jerusalem wrote in the most critical period: as Israel was annexed by Assyria (2 Kings 17), and Judaea became a tributary to the same empire (2 Chron. 28.21). He obviously knew of the 722 conquest of Israel and its dispersion. This Isaiah seems either dogmatically dependent on Amos, or is responding to similar circumstances with a similar ideology: i.e.,. to maintain the covenant with God the people were to treat others justly and not to depend on the cult and its practices.

❖ "Then I heard the voice of the Lord saying, 'Whom shall I send, and who will go for us?' And I said, 'Here I am; send me!' ...And I said: 'Woe is me! I am lost, for I am a man of unclean lips, and I live among a people of unclean lips; yet my eyes have seen of host's'" (6.8,5).

❖ "He shall judge between the nations, and shall arbitrate for many peoples; they shall beat their swords into plowshares, and their spears into pruning hooks; nation shall not lift up sword against nation, neither shall they learn war any more" (2.4).

❖ "Ah, sinful nation, people laden with iniquity, offspring who do evil, children who deal corruptly, who have forsaken the LORD, who have despised the Holy One of Israel, who are utterly estranged!" (1.4).

❖ "When you come to appear before me, who asked this from your hand? Trample my courts no more; bringing offerings is futile; incense is an abomination to me. New moon and Sabbath and calling of convocation – I cannot endure solemn assemblies with iniquity. Your new moons and your appointed festivals my soul hates; they have become a burden to me, I am weary of bearing them. When you stretch out your hands, I will hide my eyes from you; even though you make many prayers, I will not listen; your hands are full of blood. Wash yourselves; make yourselves clean; remove the evil of your doings from before my eyes; cease to do evil, learn to do good; seek justice, rescue the oppressed, defend the orphan, plead for the widow. Come now, let us argue it out, says the LORD: though your sins are like scarlet, they shall be like snow; though they are red like crimson, they shall become like wool. If you are willing and obedient, you shall eat the good of the land; but if you refuse and rebel, you shall be devoured by the sword" (1.12-20).

JEREMIAH

Jeremiah flourished as a prophet during the greatest crisis of Israelite society - at least as he viewed it.

Over 100 years earlier, Assyria had conquered the ten northern tribes. Most of their population was taken into exile and absorbed into Assyrian society and culture. They were lost as an identifiable people.

Jeremiah believed that with the rise of the new Babylonian empire the same fate was facing Judaea. Survival of his people became his purpose. He proposed political strategies and ideologies to insure that survival. While his goal was secular, he used both secular and sacred language to promote his program.

The rhetoric of these interpreters of the time was sacred in tone. Those who proposed specific programs proclaimed that they came directly from God. Whether these prophets believed that God spoke to them, or they affected this rhetorical style for secular effect, cannot be determined. However, it is clear that the effect of their pronouncements was secular.

Having come from a priestly family and called by God from childhood, Jeremiah would have come to see himself as a spokesman for God:

> "Now the word of the Lord came to me saying, 'Before I formed you in the womb I knew you, and before you were born I consecrated you; I appointed you a prophet to the nations.'" (Jer.`1.1, 4f.).

We do not know the exact historical context of the revelations for many of the prophets. However, in Jeremiah's case, the context is clear. The scene had been set when Josiah, king of Judaea (640-609), was killed in 609 by Pharaoh Necho. Josiah challenged Necho as that pharaoh was marching north from Egypt to assist Assyria in its struggle against an emerging power: the new Babylonian empire.

General political chaos and jockeying for power followed until Babylonia conquered of Judaea in 586. After Josiah's death, his son, Jehoabaz, served for three months. Necho, who enthroned his older brother, Jehoiakim, then deposed him and Judaea became an Egyptian vassal. Egypt was then weakened in 605 when Necho was defeated at Carchemish by Nebuchadnezzar, Emperor of Babylonia.

After being a vassal to Babylonia for several years, Judaea rebelled with its king, Jehoiachin, bearing the consequences of their rebellion. Nebuchadnezzar attacked Jerusalem in 598, looted the palace and Temple and exiled many of the elite. Jehoiachin's uncle, Zedekiah, although he was serving as Babylonia's surrogate vassal-ruler, was in league with Egypt, and again rebelled. Nebuchadnezzar returned once again and, after a prolonged siege, conquered Jerusalem in 586. He destroyed the Temple, executed the king's sons and blinded the king, and took him into exile with most of the other survivors. (This history is recorded in II Kings 22-25 and parallel passages in Jeremiah 21-24.10).

It was in this chaotic political environment that Jeremiah developed his program of redemption. He seems to have been a leader of a group that was convinced Judaea could not effectively resist the Babylonian Empire. They were convinced that opposition would lead to a fate similar to that the Ten Tribes of Israel suffered in 722 conquest and dispersal with a forever-loss of identity.

The opposition to Jeremiah was comprised of kings, bureaucrats, priests and prophets who sought independence from Babylonia through the assistance of Egypt. The dialogue between Hananiah, a prophet aligned with King Zedekiah, illustrates their conflict. In August of 594, he predicted the imminent end of Babylonia:

> "Thus says the Lord of hosts, the God of Israel: I have broken the yoke of the king of Babylon. Within two years I will bring back to this place all the vessels of the Lord's house, which King Nebuchadnezzar, of Babylon took away from this place and carried to Babylon ...for I will break the yoke of the king of Babylon." (Jer.28. 2-4)

Jeremiah countered with these words:

> "...the word of the Lord came to Jeremiah: Go, tell Hananiah, Thus says the Lord: You have broken wooden bars only to forge iron bars in the place of them! For thus says the Lord of hosts, the God of Israel: I have put an iron yoke on the neck of

all these nations so that they may serve King Nebuchadnezzar, of Babylon, and they shall indeed serve him; I have even given him the wild animals. And the prophet Jeremiah said to the prophet Hananiah, 'Listen, Hananiah, the Lord has not sent you, and you made this people trust in a lie. Therefore thus says the Lord: I am going to send you off the face of the earth. Within this year you will be dead, because you have spoken rebellion against the Lord.'" (Jer. 28.12-17).

Hananiah died two months later; Babylon conquered and remained dominant until 538, when Persia led by Cyrus the Great, became the region's new dominant power. Jeremiah was prescient: Egypt could not help and Babylon would prevail: Jeremiah therefore was a 'true' prophet and would be seen as the prophet through whom God spoke.

"How lightly you gad about, changing your ways! You shall be put to shame by Egypt as you were put to shame by Assyria. From there also you will come away with your hands on your head; for the Lord has rejected those in whom you trust, and you will not prosper through them " (2.36f.).

"The word of the Lord came to me a second time, saying, 'What do you see?' And I said, 'I see a boiling pot, tilted away from the north (Babylon)'" (1.13).

God is seen as in charge of history and Nebuchadnezzar, as God's servant:

"The Lord of hosts, the God of Israel, said: 'See, I am bringing punishment upon Amon of Thebes, and Pharaoh, and Egypt and her gods and her kings, upon Pharaoh and those who trust in him. I will deliver them over to those who seek their lives, to King Nebuchadnezzar, of Babylon and his officers'" (46.25f.).

Because Jeremiah's predictions went counter to the will of the establishment, he was roundly condemned and threatened:

"The priests and the prophets and all the people heard Jeremiah speaking these words in the house of the Lord. Now the Shephatiah son of Mattan, son of Shelemiah, and Pashhur son of Malchiah heard the words that Jeremiah was saying to all the people. Thus says the Lord, Those who stay in this city shall die by the sword, by famine, and by pestilence; but those who go out to the Chaldeans shall live; they shall have their lives as a prize of war, and live. Thus says the Lord, This city shall surely be handed over to the army of the king of Babylon and be taken, 'This man ought to be put to death, because he is discouraging the soldiers who are left in this city, and all the people, by speaking such words to them. For this man is not seeking the welfare of this people, but their harm.' King Zedekiah said, 'Here he is; he is in your hands; for the king is powerless against you.' So they took Jeremiah and threw him into the cistern of Malchiah, the king's son, which was in the court of the guard, letting Jeremiah down by ropes. Now there was no water in the cistern, but only mud, and Jeremiah sank in the mud" (38:1-6).

Similarly, during the reign of Jehoiakim:

"and when Jeremiah finished speaking all that the Lord had commanded him to speak to all the people, then the priests and the prophets and all the people laid hold of him, saying, 'You shall die! Why have you prophesied in the name of the Lord, saying, This house (the Temple) shall be like Shiloh (destroyed), and this city shall be desolate, without inhabitant?' And all the people gathered around Jeremiah in the house of the Lord" (26.7-9).

Jeremiah was clear as to what God demanded of the people if they were to avoid conquest by their enemies, and avoid entangling foreign alliances with their neighbors and Egypt:

"For if you truly amend your ways and your doings, if you truly act justly with one another, if you do not oppress the alien, the orphan, and the widow, or shed innocent blood in this place, and if you do not go after other gods to your own hurt, then I will dwell with you in his place, in the land I gave of old to your ancestors forever and ever. Here you are, trusting in deceptive words to no avail. Will you steal, murder, commit adultery, swear falsely, make offerings to Baal, and go after other gods that you have not known, and then come and stand before me in this house and say, 'We are safe!' -- only to go on doing these abominations? Has this house, which is called by my name, become a house of robbers in your sight? You know that I am watching, says the Lord" (7.5-11).

Typical of the leaders' hypocrisy was their freeing of their Hebrew slaves as the Babylonians were besieging Jerusalem to gain their assistance, only to rescind this freedom when an approaching Egyptian army caused the Babylonians to temporarily leave (34.8-22; 37.6-15).

Although the people did not listen to Jeremiah, in order to vindicate God they had to be warned:

> "So, says the Lord, you Jeremiah shall speak all these words to them but they will not listen to you. You shall call to them, but they will not answer you. You shall say to them: this is the nation that did not obey the voice of the Lord their God, and did not accept discipline; truth has perished; it is cut off from their lips" (7.27f.).

While Jeremiah used sacred language and invoked God to lead Judaea to purely secular goals of social justice and survival, he realized that society mainly felt that it could utilize the traditional cult and its institutions for salvation. Jeremiah makes clear that this would not work: their doom is fixed if they do not follow God's (secular) demands. Jeremiah goes so far as to deny that, during the Exodus, God gave them the Temple's sacrificial cult:

> "Thus says the Lord of hosts, the God of Israel: Add your burnt offerings to your sacrifices, and eat the flesh. For on the day that I brought your ancestors out of the land of Egypt, I did not speak to them or command them concerning burnt offerings and sacrifices. But this is the command I gave them, 'Obey my voice, and I will be your God, and you shall be my people; and walk only in the way that I command you, so that it may be well with you.' Yet they did not obey or incline their ear, but, in the stubbornness of the evil will, they walked in their own counsels, and looked backward rather than forward...they did worse than their ancestors did" (7.21-26).

And further:

> "Of what use to me is frankincense that comes from Sheba, or sweet cane from a distant land? Your burnt offerings are not acceptable, nor are your sacrifices pleasing to me" (6.20).

The Temple, the center of the cult and the priesthood, a special place proposed by David and built by Solomon, would not provide security, though it was viewed as the special abode of God:

"Do not trust in these deceptive words: 'This is the temple of
the Lord, the temple of the Lord, the temple of the Lord'"
(7.4).

As God had made clear through Jeremiah, only justice and a sensible
foreign policy would insure the nation's survival. But the leaders and
possibly a majority of others would not listen and change. Jeremiah
prophesied in his vision of the broken jug that Judaea was doomed (19).
Adherence to the cult was no substitute for morality and justice.

If there were to be a saving remnant, it would be found among
those who had been taken into exile. Jeremiah offered a revolutionary
strategy for the dispersed exiles, a strategy that has served Jews to this
day:

"These are the words of the letter that the prophet Jeremiah
sent from Jerusalem to the remaining elders among the exiles,
and to the priests, the prophets, and all the people, whom
Nebuchadnezzar, had taken into exile from Jerusalem to
Babylon. Thus says the Lord of hosts, the God of Israel, to all
the exiles whom I have sent into exile from Jerusalem to
Babylon: Build houses and live in them; plant gardens and eat
what they produce. Take wives and have sons and daughters;
take wives for your sons, and give your daughters in marriage,
that they may bear sons and daughters; multiply here, and do
not decrease. But seek the welfare of the city where I have
sent you into exile, and pray to the Lord on its behalf, for in its
welfare you will find your welfare. For thus says the Lord of
hosts, the God of Israel: Do not let the prophets and the
diviners who are among you deceive you, and do not listen to
the dreams that they dream, for it is a lie that they are
prophesying to you in my name; I did not send them, says the
Lord.
"For thus says the Lord: Only when Babylon's seventy years
are completed will I visit you, and I will fulfill to you my
promise and bring you back to this place. For surely I know
the plans I have for you, says the Lord, plans for your welfare
and not for harm, to give you a future with hope. Then when
you call upon me and come and pray to me, I will hear you.
When you search for me, you will find me; if you seek me

with all your heart, I will let you find me, says the Lord, and I will restore your fortunes and gather you from all the nations and all the places where I have driven you, says the Lord, and I will bring you back to the place from which I sent you into exile" (29.4-14).

The exiles were not to despair, but to continue with the hope that they would be restored eventually to their homeland. They were to get on with their lives, to plant and reap, to marry and bear children, and -- most amazingly -- to pray for the welfare of those who conquered and exiled them for, after all, this was part of God's plan. Their society had sinned and God sent Babylon to carry out his punishment. Babylonia would meet its fate some seventy years later when conquered by Persia. Meanwhile, it had served God's purpose.

As has been noted, Jeremiah's program was secular, couched in sacred terminology. His goal was: survival of Judaeans. In this strategy he, among others, explained to the people what had happened to them and motivated them to remain a special, identifiable group…a light unto the nations.

OTHER PRE-EXILIC PROPHETS

HOSEA, around 730, shortly after Amos, began his prophecies. Israel was suffering from a war with Assyria, and from general anarchy. In the 14 years following the death of Jeroboam II, it had had four kings. Post-Jeroboam society was not as confident as it had been during Amos' time. Now there were social and political adversities; worship of Baal was increasing; Yahweh was being worshipped only to protect special interests of the affluent and powerful. Hosea spoke against the cultic and political sins of that society. While he anticipated a hopeful renewal, it would come only after national destruction and a social purgation.

Hosea is another prophet who didn't favor the sacrificial cult:

"For I (God) desire steadfast love and not sacrifice, the knowledge of God rather than burnt offerings." (Hosea 6.6).

God's judgment was clear:

"You have plowed wickedness, you have reaped injustice, you have eaten the fruit of lies. Because you have trusted in your power and in the multitude of your warriors, therefore the tumult of war shall rise against your people, and all your fortresses shall be destroyed, as Shalman destroyed Beth-arbel on the day of battle when mothers were dashed in pieces with their children. Thus it shall be done to you, O Bethel, because of your great wickedness. At dawn the king of Israel shall be utterly cut off" (10.13-15).

But hope gleams through:

"Return, O Israel, to the Lord your God, for you have stumbled because of your iniquity. Take words with you and return to the Lord; say to him, 'Take away all guilt; accept that which is good, and we will offer the fruit of our lips. Assyria shall not save us; we will not ride upon horses; we will say no more, 'Our God,' to the work of our hands. In you the orphan finds mercy.' I will heal their disloyalty; I will love them freely, for my anger has turned from them" (14.1-4). "Those who are wise understand these things; those who are discerning know them. For the ways of the Lord are right, and the upright walk in them, but transgressors stumble in them" (14.9).

MICAH

Micah was a commoner from the small village of Moresheth, just southwest of Jerusalem and a younger contemporary of Isaiah of Jerusalem.

After Senacharib's invasion of 701, Judaea was now a weak vassal state of Assyria. The populace was to be punished for their sins. His message was unwelcomed:

"'Do not preach' – thus they preach – 'one should not preach such things; disgrace will not overtake us'" (Micah 2.6).

As with the other pre-exilic prophets, the sins of the people were chiefly social.

"And I said: Listen, you heads of Jacob and rulers of the house of Israel! Should you not know justice? – you who hate the good and love the evil, who tear the skin off my people, and the flesh off their bones; who eat the flesh of my people, flay their skin off them, break their bones in pieces, and chop them up like meat in a kettle, like flesh in a caldron. Then they will cry to the Lord, but he will not answer them; he will hide his face from them at that time, because they have acted wickedly" (3.1-4).

Those who mistreat the people but particularly the leaders would bring about the destruction of Jerusalem.

"Hear this, you rulers of the house of Jacob and chiefs of the house of Israel, who abhor justice and pervert all equity, who build Zion with blood and Jerusalem with wrong! Its rulers give judgment for a bribe, its priests teach for a price, its prophets give oracles for money; yet they lean upon the Lord and say, 'Surely the Lord is with us! No harm shall come upon us.' Therefore because of you Zion shall be plowed as a field; Jerusalem shall become a heap of ruins, and the mountain of the house a wooded height" (3.9-12).

The prophet is clear about God's desires.

"With what shall I come before the Lord, and bow myself before God on high? Shall I come before him with burnt offerings, with calves a year old? Will the Lord be pleased with thousands of rams, with ten thousands of rivers of oil? Shall I give my firstborn for my transgression, the fruit of my body for the sin of my soul? He has told you, O mortal, what is good; and what does the Lord require of you but to do justice, and to love kindness, and to walk humbly with your God" (6.6-8).

Micah (or someone else with a more optimistic message) had high hopes for the future; a messianic future. Not only would the Judaeans be restored, all others would turn to God.

"In days to come the mountain of the Lord's house shall be established as the highest of the mountains, and shall be raised up above the hills. Peoples shall stream to it, and many nations shall come and say: 'Come, let us go up to the mountain of the Lord, to the house of the God of Jacob; that he may teach us his ways and that we may walk in his paths.' For out of Zion shall go forth instruction, and the word of the Lord from Jerusalem. He shall judge between many peoples, and shall arbitrate between strong nations far away; they shall beat their swords into plowshares, and their spears in pruning hooks; nation shall not lift up sword against nation, neither shall they learn war any more; but they shall all sit under their own vines and under their own fig trees, and no one shall make them afraid; for the mouth of the Lord of hosts has spoken. For all the peoples walk, each in the name of its god, but we will walk in the name of the Lord our God forever and ever. In that day, says the Lord, I will assemble the lame and gather those who have been driven away, and those whom I have afflicted. The lame I will make the remnant, and those who were cast off, a strong nation; and the Lord will reign over them in Mount Zion now and forevermore" (4.1-7).

NAHUM

Nahum flourished between 626 and 612. He rejoiced at the defeat of the Assyrians by the Medes of northern Persia and the Chaldeans of southern Babylonia. Asshur fell in 614 and Nineveh in 612.

Nahum was convinced that the defeat of Assyria was accomplished by God's judgment on an unscrupulous, defiant nation. God's power would fulfill the secular aim of making Judaea safe.

❖ "An oracle concerning Nineveh. The book of the vision of Nahum of Elkosh. A jealous and avenging God is the Lord, the Lord is avenging and wrathful; the Lord takes vengeance on his adversaries and rages against his enemies" (1.1-2).

❖ "A shatterer has come up against you. Guard the ramparts; watch the road; gird your loins; collect all your strength" (2.1).

❖ "Ah! City of bloodshed, utterly deceitful, full of booty – no end to the plunder! The crack of whip and rumble of wheel, galloping horse and bounding chariot! Horsemen charging, flashing sword and glittering spear, piles of dead, heaps of corpses, dead bodies without end – they stumble over the bodies" (3.1-3).

❖ "Then all who see you will shrink from you and say, 'Nineveh is devastated; who will bemoan her?' Where shall I seek comforters for you?" (3.7).

❖ "Your shepherds are asleep, O king of Assyria; your nobles slumber. Your people are scattered on the mountains with no one to gather them" (3.18).

❖ "Look! On the mountains the feet of one who brings good tidings, who proclaims peace! Celebrate your festivals, O Judah, fulfill your vows, for never again shall the wicked invade you; they are utterly cut off" (1.15).

HABAKKUK

During the height of Babylonian power, Habakkuk prophesied from 608 on. The prophet sought an answer to the plight of the Judaeans, possibly just after the exile of 597 and the generally deteriorating conditions of the society. He seems to be challenging God:

"Your eyes are too pure to behold evil, and you cannot look on wrongdoing; why do you look on the treacherous, and are silent when the wicked swallow those more righteous than they?"(1.13) .

An answer is that eventually the righteous will be vindicated.

"Look at the proud! Their spirit is not right in them, but the righteous live by their faith" (2.4).

Wickedness within society will be followed by conquest by Babylonia.

"Oh Lord, how long shall I cry for help, and you will not listen? Or cry to you 'Violence!' and you will not save? Why do you make me see wrongdoing and look at trouble? Destruction and violence are before me; strife and contention arise. So the law becomes slack and justice never prevails. The wicked surround the righteous – therefore judgment comes forth perverted. For I am rousing the Chaldean, that fierce and impetuous nation, who march through the breadth of the earth to seize dwellings not their own. Dread and fearsome are they; their justice and dignity proceed from themselves" (1.2-4; 6-7).

Yet, even as conditions remain perilous in this dark period, the people maintain hope.

"Though the fig tree does not blossom, and no fruit is on the vines; though the produce of the olive fails and the fields yield no food; though the flock is cut off from the fold and there is no herd in the stalls, yet I will rejoice in the Lord; I will exult in the God of my salvation. God, the Lord, is my strength; he makes my feet like the feet of a deer, and makes me tread upon the heights" (3.17-19).

ZEPHANIAH

Zephaniah the great grandson of King Hezekiah, was descended from the royal family. He prophesied about 630.

"The word of the Lord that came to Zephaniah son of Cushi son of Gedaliah son of Amariah son of Hezekiah, in the days of King Josiah son of Amon of Judah" (1.1). The upper classes are corrupt and will be destroyed.

The prophet uses cultic language for secular ends.

"Be silent before the Lord God! For the day of the Lord is at hand; the Lord has prepared a sacrifice, he has consecrated his guests. And on the day of the Lord's sacrifice I will punish the officials and the king's sons and all who dress themselves in foreign attire. On that day I will punish all who leap over the threshold, who fill their master's house with violence and fraud. On that day, says the Lord, a cry will be heard from the Fish Gate, a wail from the Second Quarter, a loud crash from the hills. The inhabitants of the Mortar wail, for all the traders have perished; all who weigh out silver are cut off. At that time I will search Jerusalem with lamps, and I will punish the people who rest complacently on their dregs, those who say in their hearts, 'The Lord will not do good, nor will he do harm.' Their wealth shall be plundered, and their houses laid waste. Though they build houses, they shall not inhabit them; though they plant vineyards, they shall not drink wine from them. The great day of the Lord is near, near and hastening fast; the sound of the day of the Lord is bitter, the warrior cries aloud there. That day will be a day of wrath, a day of distress and anguish, a day of ruin and devastation, a day of darkness and gloom, a day of clouds and thick darkness, a day of trumpet blast and battle cry against the fortified cities and against the lofty battlements" (1.7-16).

However, there is hope for the lower classes.

"On that day you shall not be put to shame because of all the deeds by which you have rebelled against me; for then I will remove from your midst your proudly exultant ones, and you shall no longer be haughty in my holy mountain. For I will leave in the midst of you a people humble and lowly. They shall seek refuge in the name of the Lord – the remnant of Israel; they shall do no wrong and utter no lies, nor shall a deceitful tongue be found in their mouths. Then they will pasture and lie down, and no one shall make them afraid" (3.11-13).

Chapter Nineteen

Herein God is universal to all
nations

JONAH

Jonah is an atypical book from the post-exilic period. It ought to be understandable why most Judaean literature following the conquest of Jerusalem, the destruction of the Temple and the exile was concerned with the survival of the Jewish people.

Jonah, however, presents an expansive look at the outside world, focusing on God's concern for the sinful people of Nineveh. Not only are they gentiles, but they are citizens of the capital city of Assyria, the hated enemy of Israel.

In this book, God instructs Jonah to go to Nineveh to warn them that their sinful ways would inflict dire punishment upon them. It is humanly logical that Jonah would resist helping the enemies of his people. After fleeing from his assignment, God instructed him a second time to go to Nineveh.

On arriving there, he warned them that in forty days – absent repentance – Nineveh would be destroyed. An amazing biblical event, in stark contradistinction to Pharaohnic Egypt, occurred. Led by their king, the people of Nineveh turned away from their evil ways. God, accordingly, changed his mind about destroying them. This turn of events angered Jonah who was also grieving that his sheltering bush dried up. God's answer to his complaint concerning the bush concludes the book:

> "And should I not be concerned about Nineveh, that great city,
> in which are more than a hundred and twenty thousand
> persons who do not know their right hand from their left and
> also many animals?" (4. 11).

From its sacred orientation, this book once again affirms the power of God. God sends Jonah on his mission; when Nineveh repents God relents and spares the city that had been sinful. Israel, vulnerable after so many defeats, required constant assurance of God's power. What better way to prove this than through his abilities to destroy and to forgive. It is a metaphor for God's forgiving his chosen, his covenanted people who repeatedly rebelled against him. We can see this as a secular element reinforcing an essential belief which would support their survival.

God being shown as universal enhances his power: he rules not only over Israel, he rules over all other nations as well.

The Hebrew Bible mixes the particular with the universal. This blend begins with Abraham, with whom God first made a covenant. Abraham and his descendants would be a blessing to all people. Amos and Isaiah of the Exile also extol God as a universal God. The greater God's power is seen to be by Israel, the more secure they would feel about what he could do for them.

Chapter Twenty
*Why Judaeans had suffered, their
bright future, and a coming
messianic age.*

ISAIAH OF THE EXILE

Judaea's defeat by Babylonia in 586 led to the exile of much of its
population. Many had already been taken in 597 with many others
fleeing into Egypt.

This terrible defeat threatened the survival of the Jewish-ness of its people.
Isaiah of the Exile (Isaiah--X) [previously termed Deutero-Isaiah] was the
primary ideologue confronting that enormous threat; Jeremiah had
explained why they were defeated and what the exiles must do as long as
the exile lasted.

     The utter-ness of their defeat in Jerusalem had precipitated a severe
crisis of belief and a challenge to the maintenance of the Judaean's special
identity[4]. Everything giving purpose and security to their lives had been
destroyed. God, with whom they had a special relationship, could be seen
as either having abandoned them in the war, or having lesser power than
Babylonia's gods.

     Their penalty seemed far greater than their sins. If this was so,
where was the justice of their God? Their Davidic monarchy had crashed
into disrepute. The Temple, the center of their religious life, was leveled.
Most of them were exiled to a foreign land, uprooted from what they had
come to believe was both holy and promised to them.

Isaiah-X formulated a brilliant response, one effective for his own time,
and, to a great extent, still operative for many Jews, today. Isaiah-X
clearly indicates that what happened to them in no way invalidated their
God or vitiated his power. God was in charge of history and remained all-
powerful. What happened to the people was caused by their sins, their
personal derelictions and shortcomings.

     The prophet clearly declares God's great power.

     "Who has measured the waters in the hollow of his hand and
     marked off the heavens with a span, enclosed the dust of the

---

[4] Not a secular tradition or monarchy: all have this. A long term residence in Canaan; the
LAW; circumcision; the oral Bible? Maybe it is Monotheism?

earth in a measure, and weighed the mountains in scales and the hills in a balance? Who has directed the spirit of the Lord, or as his counselor has instructed him? Whom did he consult for his enlightenment, and who taught him the path of justice? Who taught him knowledge, and showed him the way of understanding? Even the nations are like a drop from a bucket, and are accounted as dust on the scales; see, he takes up the isles like fine dust. Lebanon would not provide fuel enough, nor are its animals enough for a burnt offering. All the nations are as nothing before him; they are accounted by him as less than nothing and emptiness. To whom then will you liken God, or what likeness compare with him?" (40.12-18).

"I am the Lord, and there is no other; besides me there is no god. I arm you, though you do not know me, so that they may know, from the rising of the sun and from the west, that there is no one besides me; I am the Lord, and there is no other. I form light and create darkness, I make weal and create woe; I the Lord do all these things" (45.5-7).

Having established the reality and power of God, Isaiah-X then explains the suffering of the people. Their questioning faith craved answers to:

- ❖ Why did they suffer?
- ❖ Would their suffering end?
- ❖ Was there a purpose to their suffering?

Isaiah-X's explanatory writings form the central motif of his work:

- ➤ "Be comforted, be comforted my people, says your God (40.1)."

He then has God declare that their suffering is over and that it was indeed more than they in usual understanding deserved:

- ➤ "Speak tenderly to Jerusalem, and cry to her that she has served her term, that her penalty is paid, that she has received from the Lord's hand double for all her sins" (40.2).

The people would be relieved to learn that their punishment had ended. But why were they punished so heavily? To answer this, the prophet developed the concept of the suffering servant: their suffering was to help others.

God chose the Jews and gave them an exalted mission: <u>to carry on God's work on earth.</u>

> "But you, Israel, my servant, Jacob, whom I have chosen, the offspring of Abraham, my friend; you whom I took from the ends of the earth, and called from its farthest corners, saying to you, 'you are my servant, I have chosen you and not cast you off; do not fear, for I am with you, do not be afraid, for I am your God; I will strengthen you, I will help you, I will uphold you with my victorious right hand. Yes, all who are incensed against you shall be ashamed and disgraced; those who strive against you shall be as nothing and shall perish. You shall seek those who contend with you, but you shall not find them; those who war against you shall be as nothing at all. For I, the Lord your God, hold your right hand; it is I who say to you, Do not fear, I will help you'" (41.8-13).

"Here is my servant, whom I uphold, my chosen, in whom my soul delights; I have put my spirit upon him; he will bring forth justice to the nations. I am the Lord, I have called you in righteousness, I have taken you by the hand and kept you; I have given you as a covenant to the people, a light to the nations, to open the eyes that are blind, to bring out the prisoners from the dungeon, from the prison those who sit in darkness" (42.1, 6-7).

What better motivation might be given to a broken people than to be told that God, THE God, himself, chose them for an exalted mission? They had to understand what had happened and why.

More importantly, however, they had to survive to carry out this mission. Isaiah-X explains why their suffering was double what one might have been expected for their sins: they were God's suffering servants. They would suffer for testifying to the one true God's existence and the morality he demanded of the faithful.

"And now the Lord says, who formed me in the womb to be his servant, to bring Jacob back to him, and that Israel might be gathered to him, for I am honored in the sight of the Lord, and my God has become my strength – he says, 'It is too light a thing that you should be my servant to raise up the tribes of Jacob and to restore the survivors of Israel; I will give you as a light to the nations, that my salvation may reach to the end of the earth.' Thus says the Lord, the Redeemer of Israel and his Holy One, to one deeply despised, abhorred by the nations, the slave of rulers, 'Kings shall see and stand up, princes, and they shall prostrate themselves, because of the Lord, who is faithful, the Holy One of Israel, who has chosen you'" (49.5-7). "See, my servant shall prosper; he shall be exalted and lifted up, and shall be very high. Just as there were many who were astonished at him – so marred was his appearance, beyond human semblance, and his form beyond that of mortals – so he shall startle many nations; kings shall shut their mouths because of him; for that which had not been told them they shall see, and that which they had not heard they shall contemplate" (52.13-15).

This concept was fully fleshed out. Israel was portrayed as despised and rejected, but ready to take whatever came its way because of its exalted role: to bear the sins of others and bring them to God, regardless of the price it must pay.

"Who has believed what we have heard? And to whom has the arm of the Lord been revealed? For he grew up before him like a young plant, and like a root out of dry ground; he had no form or majesty that we should look at him, nothing in his appearance that we should desire him. He was despised and rejected by others; a man of suffering and acquainted with infirmity; and as one from whom others hide their faces. He was despised and we held him of no account. Surely he has borne our infirmities and carried our diseases; yet we accounted him stricken, struck down by God, and afflicted. But he was wounded for our transgressions, crushed for our iniquities; upon him was the punishment that made us whole, and by his bruises we are healed. All we like sheep have gone astray; we have all turned to our own way, and the Lord has laid on him the iniquity of us all. He was oppressed, and he was afflicted, yet he did not open his mouth; like a lamb that is led to the slaughter, and like a sheep that before its shearers is silent, so he did not open his mouth. By a perversion of justice he was taken away. Who could have imagined his future? For he was cut off from the land of the living, stricken for the transgression of my people. They made his grave with the wicked and his tomb with the rich, although he had done no violence and there was no deceit in his mouth. Yet it was the will of the Lord to crush him with pain. When you make his life an offering for sin, he shall see his offspring, and shall prolong his days; through him the will of the Lord shall prosper. Out of his anguish he shall see light; he shall find satisfaction through his knowledge. The righteous one, my servant, shall make many righteous, and he shall bear their iniquities. Therefore I will allot him a portion with the great, and he shall divide the spoil with the strong; because he poured out himself to death, and was numbered with the transgressors; yet he bore the sins of many, and made intercession for the transgressors" (53.1-12).

With these explanations for what befell the Judaeans, and for their relationship with God and with others, there remained another crucial challenge for the creativity of Isaiah-X and his ideology: what would the future bring? The answer was simple: It would be wonderful. God's power would be reasserted in history, as those who conquered them would be conquered. God was in charge of history. The preeminent enemy, Babylon, would be defeated.

"Come down and sit in the dust, virgin daughter Babylon! Sit on the ground without a throne, daughter Chaldea! For you shall no more be called tender and delicate. Take the millstones and grind meal, remove your veil, strip off your robe, uncover your legs, pass through the rivers. Your nakedness shall be uncovered, and your shame shall be seen, I will take vengeance, and I will spare no one" (47.1-4).

They would be replaced by one of God's choosing: "Thus says the Lord to his anointed, to Cyrus (538), whose right hand I have grasped to subdue the nations before him and strip kings of their robes, to open doors before him -- and the gates shall not be closed" (45.1).

Other passages also pointed to a great future, a messianic age, a utopian time where peace and prosperity would reign. These visions certainly gave Isaiah-X's auditors something positive to look forward to. The messianic vision would develop around the figure of David, the ideal king.

✓ "A shoot shall come out from the stump of Jesse, and a branch shall grow out of his roots. The spirit of the Lord shall rest on him, the spirit of wisdom and understanding, the spirit of counsel and might, the spirit of knowledge and the fear of the Lord" (11.1-3).

✓ "On that day the root of Jesse shall stand as a signal to the peoples; the nations shall inquire of him, and his dwelling shall be glorious. On that day the Lord will extend his hand yet a second time to recover the remnant that is left of his people, from Assyria, from Egypt, from Pathros, from Ethiopia, from Elam, from Shinar, from Hamath, and from the coastlands of the sea" (11.10-11).

Other messianic visions abound.

✓ "The spirit of the Lord God is upon me, because the Lord has anointed me; he has sent me to bring good news to the oppressed, to bind up the brokenhearted, to proclaim liberty to the captives, and release to the prisoners...they shall repair the ruined cities, the devastations of many generations" (61.1-6).

✓ "He shall judge between the nations, and shall arbitrate for many peoples; they shall beat their swords into plowshares, and their spears into pruning hooks; nation shall not life up sword against nation, neither shall they learn war any more" (2.4).

✓ "A voice cries out: 'In the wilderness prepare the way of the Lord, make straight in the desert a highway for our God. Every valley shall be lifted up, and every mountain and hill be made low; the uneven ground shall become level, and the rough places a plain. Then the glory of the Lord shall be revealed, and all people shall see it together, for the mouth of the Lord has spoken'" (40.3-5).

✓ "See, the Lord God comes with might, and his arm rules for him; his reward is with him, and his recompense before him. He will feed his flock like a shepherd; he will gather the lambs in his arms, and carry them in his bosom, and gently lead the mother sheep" (40.10-11).

There would be special compensation: "Because their shame was double, and dishonor was proclaimed as their lot, therefore they shall possess a double portion; everlasting joy shall be theirs" (61.7).

So great will their future be that gentiles will become Jewish: indeed, 'my house shall be a house of prayer for all peoples.'

"And the foreigners who join themselves to the Lord, to minister to him, to love the name of the Lord, and to be his servants, all who keep the Sabbath, and do not profane it, and hold fast my covenant – these I will bring to my holy mountain, and make them joyful in my house of prayer; their burnt offerings and their sacrifices will be accepted on my altar; for my house shall be called a house of prayer for all peoples. Thus says the Lord God, who gathers the outcasts of Israel, I will gather others to them besides those already gathered" (56.6-8).

In 538, Cyrus, King of Persia, defeated Babylonia and eventually allowed Judaean exiles to return to their homeland. Of Cyrus, God states,

"he is my shepherd, and he shall carry out all my purpose."
(44.28)

This purpose included the rebuilding of Jerusalem and the Temple.

For Isaiah-X's agenda, it was essential that God be central to his ideology. However, Isaiah's purpose, was essentially secular: Preserving the Identity of his People. While Israel would be seen as chosen by God, their mission was purely secular, as noted in the mission passages. This mission was reinforced by their belief in God, his power and his special tie and promises with and to Israel.

Chapter Twenty-One
*Prophets of and after the exile have
very similar sacred messages,
many with the promise of a
messiah.*

OTHER POST-EXILIC PROPHETS

Jeremiah and Isaiah of the Exile developed unique responses to the disaster of 586, and the Babylonian conquest of Judaea and the exile of most of its populace. Their philosophies for survival were so effective that their essential elements still live on in Judaism.

Other post-exilic prophets dealt with the catastrophe, with messages that resemble each other:
- God would restore the exiles to the Promised Land;
- they would primarily relate to him by means of the sacrificial cult in a rebuilt Temple;
- God's great power would humble Israel's enemies;
- Israel would enjoy a glorious future.

The restored community as thus envisioned would be thoroughly sacralized. The Temple (together with some other emerging ideas) would return the people's identity to a religious focus, rather than part of a secular state supported by a priesthood and cult.

From the time of Alexander the Great, with the exception of the Hasmonean Monarchy, which lasted for some eighty years (from 140 until 60) as an independent entity, the Jewish people did not have a nation-state until some 2300 years later. Between times, religion became the raison d'être for their sense of meaning: unity and survival.

EZEKIEL

By far the lengthiest book of the Prophets, Ezekiel is filled with oracles:
- of judgment against Jerusalem and Israel,
- against other nations,
- and (in conclusion) of hope and the restoration of Jerusalem, with Israel as the center of the world.

The best-known expression of this is the Vision of the Valley of Dry Bones:

"Therefore prophesy, and say to them, Thus says the Lord God: I am going to open your graves, and bring you up from your graves, O my people; and I will bring you back to the land of Israel. And you shall know that I am the Lord, when I open your graves, and bring you up from your graves, O my people. I will put my spirit within you, and you shall live, and I will place you on your own soil; then you shall know that I, the Lord have spoken and will act, says the Lord" (37. 12-14).

In this entirely new epoch, God will give them a new spirit and replace their heart of stone with a heart of flesh. A new Israel, unlike its ancestors, will then be obedient to God (11.19-21).

Hope was essential for the people to continue as Jews. Destruction and exile tragedies posed these troublesome questions: Why would God allow this to happen? What future would they have? The answers are contained elsewhere in the Hebrew Bible: the people sinned, but their reformation with God's mercy would lead to a restoration; the people would then uphold the covenant in the land of Israel. Ezekiel emphasized that the Temple was the central institution with purity, sacrifices and observance of the holidays as ways to rid themselves of their failures and guilt. The priests had to be loyal to God, and any future king would be subservient to the priesthood.

Ezekiel contains apocalypses, cryptic symbolic narratives that are emblematic of the post-exilic period. In the last six chapters of Daniel, God revealed his end of days plan wherein the enemies of Israel would be destroyed and Israel would prosper. The world is now sacralized with supernatural intervention in the interest of Israel's secular goal: Survival of an Identifiable, Viable Community.

HAGGAI

After Cyrus the Great allowed the Israelites to return to Judaea, in 538 he encouraged them to rebuild the Temple (Ezra 1. 1-4), but by 520 little had been accomplished. Those who returned were concerned with reestablishing themselves.

God remonstrated:

"...my house lies in ruins, while all of you hurry off to your own houses" (1. 7-9).

Haggai exhorted Zerubbabel (the assigned governor) and Joshua (the high priest) to get on with the job. He conveys his message to them and the people in five addresses. Haggai observed that God would take care of them - as he'd promised during the Exodus. Furthermore, he predicted apocalyptic events leading to a messianic period with God establishing Zerubbabel as king on the throne of David:

> "For thus says the Lord of hosts: Once again, in a little while, I will shake the earth and the sea and the dry land; and I will shake all the nations, so that the treasure of all nations shall come, and I will fill this house with splendor, says the Lord of hosts...On that day, says the Lord of hosts, I will take you, O Zerubbabel my servant, son of Shealtiel, says the Lord, and make you a signet ring; for I have chosen you, says the Lord of hosts" (2. 6-7, 23).

Haggai was convinced their new situation required a sacralized setting. He was successful. By 515, while the general population was getting on with its secular affairs, the Temple had been reconstructed.

JOEL

Joel continues to prophesy in Haggai's mode. The Israelites were punished by an army sent by God, bringing them to the brink of obliteration. After a return to God with fasting and lamenting, salvation and an ideal future would follow. The destruction shall result in:

> "Blow the trumpet in Zion; sound the alarm on my holy mountain! Let all the inhabitants of the land tremble, for the day of the Lord is coming, it is near, a day of darkness and gloom, a day of clouds and thick darkness! Like the blackness spread upon the mountains a great and powerful army comes; their like has never been from of old, nor will be again after them in ages to come" (2. 1-2).

God's implied forgiveness and call to return:

> "Yet even now, says the Lord, return to me with all your heart, with fasting, with weeping, with mourning; rend your hearts and not your clothing. Return to the Lord, your God, for he is gracious and merciful, slow to anger, and abounding in steadfast love, and relents from punishing" (2. 12-13).

Hope is provided by the assurance that such disasters would never occur again:

"You shall eat in plenty and be satisfied, and praise the name of the Lord your God, who has dealt wondrously with you. And my people shall never again be put to shame. You shall know that I am in midst of Israel, and that I, the Lord, am your God and there is no other. And my people shall never again be put to shame" (2. 26-27). This assurance is reinforced by a vision of the defeat of Israel's enemies and its eternal survival: "Egypt shall become a desolation and Edom a desolate wilderness, because of the violence done to the people of Judaea, in whose land they have shed innocent blood. But Judaea shall be inhabited forever, and Jerusalem to all generations" (3. 19-20).

ZECHARIAH

Zechariah repeats the essence of what had become the mantra of the post-exilic prophets: a totally sacralized society! It was to result from Israelite awareness that their sinfulness led to their defeat and exile, and that a renewed loyalty to God (and a restored Temple cult) would result in a glorious future. Zechariah cited to them the cause for their punishment:

> "Thus says the Lord of hosts: Return to me, says the Lord of hosts, and I will return to you, says the Lord of hosts. Do not be like your ancestors, to whom the former prophets proclaimed, thus says the Lord of hosts, return from you evil ways and from your evil deeds. But they did not hear or heed me, says the Lord" (1. 3-4).

Awareness of their situation altered their behavior:

> "Your ancestors, where are they? And the prophets, do they live forever? But my words and my statutes, which I commanded my servants, the prophets, did they not overtake your ancestors? So they repented and said, 'The Lord of hosts has dealt with us according to our ways and deeds, just as he planned to do'" (1. 5-6).

God would take care of them:

> "Just as you have been cursing among the nations, O house of Judah and house of Israel, so I will save you and you shall be a blessing. Do not be afraid, but let your hands be strong. For thus says the Lord of hosts: Just as I proposed to bring disaster upon you, when your ancestors provoked me to wrath, and I

did not relent, says the Lord of hosts, so again I have proposed
in these days to do good to Jerusalem and the house of Judah;
do not be afraid" (8. 13-15).

Zechariah projects an ideal future: a messianic age when Israel will be
protected, an age of all peoples acknowledging God:

"And God will give victory to the tents of Judaea first, that the
glory of the house of David and the glory of the inhabitants of
Jerusalem may not be exalted over that of Judaea. On that day
the Lord will shield the inhabitants of Jerusalem so that the
feeblest among them on that day shall be like David, and the
house of David shall be like God, like the angel of the Lord, at
their head. And on that day I will seek to destroy all the
nations that come against Jerusalem...And it shall be
inhabited, for never again shall it be doomed to destruction;
Jerusalem shall abide in security ...And the Lord will become
king over the earth; on that day the Lord shall be one and his
name one" (12.7-9; 14. 11, 9).

MALACHI

Malachi, also a cultic prophet, harshly criticizes the priesthood:

"despised" God's name and led the people astray. The loyal
priests "had true instruction on (their) lips and walked with
(God) in integrity and uprightness, and turned away from
iniquity. For the lips of a priest should guard knowledge, and
people should seek instruction from his mouth , for he is the
messenger of the Lord of hosts" (2. 6-7).

It was up to God to accomplish this. Apparently, Malachi felt that the
Levites weren't up to doing it on their own:

"For he is like a refiner's fire and like fuller's soap; he will sit
as a refiner and purifier of silver, and he will purify the
descendants of Levi and refine them like gold and silver, until
they present offerings to the Lord in righteousness. Then the
offering of Judaea and Jerusalem will be pleasing to the Lord
as in the days of old and as in former years" (3. 2b-4).

Once again, God is portrayed as prepared to clear the path for a glorious
future:

"See, the day is coming, burning like an oven, when all the arrogant and evildoers will be stubble; the day that comes shall burn them up, says the Lord of hosts, so that it will leave them neither root nor branch, but for you who revere my name, the sun of righteousness shall rise, with healing on its wings. You shall go out leaping like calves from the stall...Lo, I will send you the prophet Elijah before the great and terrible day of the Lord comes. He will turn the hearts of the parents to their children and the hearts of the children to their parents, so that I will not come and strike the land with a curse" (4.1-2, 5).

In addition, all peoples will acknowledge God:

"From the rising of the sun to its setting my name is great among the nations...for I am a great King, says the Lord of hosts, and my name is reverenced among the nations" (1. 11a, 14b).

NAHUM

Nahum uses Nineveh as the paradigm for sinfulness and God's presence in history. For Israel, that overbearing and exceedingly oppressive Nineveh symbolized sinfulness. On account of Nineveh's behavior, it was to be totally destroyed and never rebuilt. This would be the fate of all evildoers - an affirmation to God's power.

Nahum's message for Israel was to obey God, but also have hope and to trust that God would rescue them from those who oppress them.

"A jealous and avenging God is the Lord, the Lord is avenging and wrathful; the Lord takes vengeance on his adversaries and rages against his enemies. The Lord is slow to anger but great in power, and the Lord will by no means clear the guilty...He will make a full end of his adversaries, and will pursue his enemies into darkness" (1. 2-3a, 8).

Great hope for the future of Israel is assured:

"Look! On the mountains the feet of one who brings good tidings, who proclaims peace! Celebrate your festivals, O Judah, fulfill your vows, for never again shall the wicked invade you; they are utterly cut off" (1. 15).

OBADIAH

Comprising just 291 Hebrew words, Obadiah stands out as the shortest book of the Hebrew Bible.

As in the other post-exilic prophetic books, the enemies of Israel are to be punished; Israel will have recompense and a good future.

> "The day of the Lord is near against all the nations. As you have done, it shall be done to you; your deeds shall return on you own head...But on Mount Zion there shall be those that escape, and it shall be holy; and the house of Jacob shall take possession of those who dispossessed them...Those who have been saved shall go up to Mount Zion to rule Mount Esau; and the kingdom shall be the Lord's" (1. 15, 17,21).

Chapter Twenty-Two
*An overview of Psalms
demonstrates their sacred rather
than secular nature.*

PSALMS

The books of Psalms is a collection of 150 poetic prayers. They were probably used liturgically in Temple worship. Their themes recapitulate many of the major themes of the Hebrew Bible:

- o God's supreme power over everything;
- o the promise to Abraham of the land and progeny;
- o the Exodus;
- o the Exile;
- o the centrality of Jerusalem, Zion and the Temple.

The psalms fall into three general categories:

1) hymns of praise,
2) complaints and pleas for help,
3) and thanksgiving.

They are essentially sacred, with God at the center, heaping praise on him for his power and beneficence, his creation of the world, and his past acts of deliverance. The major activity of humans is to praise God and to envision a world where all people will do so. A major shift in these poems from national to personal concerns is notable.

A few examples exemplify these themes.

a) The 23rd Psalm, the best known, begins with "The Lord is my shepherd, I shall not want" (23.1) It sets the stage for the many themes of the psalms.

b) "It is good to give thanks to the Lord, to sing praises to your name, O most high" (92.2).

c) "Happy is everyone who fears the Lord, who walks in his ways" (128.1).

d) "Out of the depths I cry to you O Lord. Lord, hear my voice! Let your ears be attentive to the voice of my supplications" (130.1).

e) "Blessed be the Lord, my rock, who trains my hands for war, and my fingers for battle; my rock and my fortress, my stronghold and my deliverer, my shield, in whom I take refuge, who subdues the peoples under me" (144. 1-2).

One essentially secular example is Psalm 72:

> while God is called upon to give justice and righteousness to the king, presumably, Solomon, the king is exhorted to help his people in specific ways for their security and prosperity (72. 2-17).

Chapter Twenty-Three

*In contradistinction to the sacred Psalms attributed
to David, the Proverbs attributed to Solomon are
essentially secular and many use feminine nouns.
Does this imply that female deities are being alluded
to?*

PROVERBS

The Book of Proverbs, as are the other books comprising the Wisdom
Literature, is attributed to Solomon:

"(Solomon) composed three thousand proverbs, and his songs
numbered a thousand and five" (I Kings 4.32).

The Hebrew word for proverb is *mashal* which means 'a saying' and by
implication 'to be similar to' and to 'rule over.' From the content of the
Proverbs it is clear that what is meant is that the reader is to rule over the
pitfalls of life, to avoid what is undesirable.

The authors of these proverbs sought to apply the disciplined
intelligence and moral experience of good people to the day-to-day
problems of ordinary people. It directed practical philosophy to seek out
satisfaction in life. There is very little herein concerning the cult, the
priesthood, the Temple, the covenant, or much about the religious ethos of
Biblical society. In the 910 verses of the collection, only 76 mention God
and many of the 76 use the idea of God to reinforce rather mundane
values. The proverbs are essentially secular, practical, didactic, and
worldly wise.

A unique element of the first nine chapters is their employment of a series
of feminine nouns. Featured is *chachmah* (wisdom). In several instances,
chachmah may be seen as deity, performing acts usually reserved for God.

"But those who listen to me (chachmah) will dwell securely
and will live at ease, without dread of disaster" (1.33). "Hear,
my son, and take my (chachmah's) sayings and the years of
your life may be many" (4.10).

Chachmah is also seen as having co-existed with God before Creation:

"I (chachmah) was set up from everlasting, from the beginning
of the earth" (7.23).

Much of the language of 8.32-36, referring to chachmah, is usually
reserved for God:

- "listen to me for happy are those who will keep my words" (32)
- "... he who finds me finds life" (35)
- "... all who hate me, love death" (36).

Other feminine nouns are used in these passages and have similar meanings:

    i.   *beena* (understanding),
    ii.   *arma* (prudence),
    iii.   *tachbala* (guidance),
    iv.   *daat* (knowledge),
    v.   *t'nuva* (discernment)
    vi.   *torah* (learning).

Many explanations for these nouns have been suggested:

- to subtly substitute for feminine deities which could no longer be worshipped;
- to wean the people from such feminine deities;
- to feature secular values.

One of the terms for God, ale shaddai, usually translated as God Almighty, literally means 'God of my breasts.' The implication is that God has a feminine, nurturing side to his/her nature. Indeed, this name is noted as anteceding God's other names:

> "God spoke to Moses and said to him: I am the Lord (Yahweh). I appeared to Abraham, Isaac and Jacob as ale shaddai, but by my name 'the Lord' I did not make myself known to them" (Exodus 6.2f.).

The feminine element in ale shaddai is clear in the passage where God is denoted in several ways:

> "Yet how taut is (Joseph's) bow and his arms were made agile by the hands of the Mighty One of Jacob, by the name of the Shepherd, the Rock of Israel, by the God of your father, who will help you, by the Shaddai (my breasts) who will bless you with blessings of heaven above, blessings of the deep that lies beneath, blessings of the shaddaim (breasts) and of the womb" (Genesis 49.24f.).

That feminine deities were worshipped by Judaeans is clear from the following passage, written in the period immediately prior to the destruction of the first Temple in Jerusalem in 586:

"Then all the men who were aware that their wives had been making offerings to other gods ... (and the women, living in Egypt, responded to the prophet, Jeremiah) 'as for the word that you have spoken to us in the name of the Lord, we are not going to listen to you. Instead, we will do everything that we have vowed, make offerings to the queen of heaven and pour our libations to her, just as we and our ancestors, our kings and our officials used to do in the towns of Judaea and in the streets of Jerusalem. But from the time we stopped making offerings to the queen of heaven and pouring out libations to her, we have lacked everything and have perished by the sword and by famine'" (Jeremiah 44.15-18).

The agenda for this collection of sayings is laid out at the beginning:
1. "to know wisdom (chachmah) and instruction;
2. to comprehend the words of understanding (beenah);
3. to receive the discipline of wisdom, righteousness, justice and equity;
4. to give prudence (arma) to the simple, to the young man knowledge (daas) and discretion (m'zeema);
5. that the wise man may hear and increase in learning;
6. to understand a proverb (mashal) and a figure; the words of the wise and their dark sayings (chidos)" (1.2-6).
   "Wisdom (chachmah) cries aloud in the street, she raises her voice in broad places... because I have called and you refused, I have stretched out my hand and no man attended; you have ignored all my counsel and would have none of my reproof" (1.20, 24).
Could the following be a contrast with negative feminine qualities?
"You will be saved from the loose woman, from the adulteress with her smooth words" (2.16).

While an overwhelming number of verses in Proverbs are secular, there are many references to God. Among the more important verses are the following:
1) "The fear of the Lord is the beginning of knowledge; but the foolish despise wisdom and discipline" (1.7).

2) "Trust in the Lord with all your heart and lean not upon your own understanding...Do not be wise in your own eyes; fear the Lord and depart from evil" (3.5, 7).

3) "For the Lord loves him whom He corrects, even as a father the son in whom he delights" (3.12).

4) "The eyes of the Lord are in every place, keeping watch upon the evil and the good" (15.3).

But most of this instruction is clearly secular, as a selection of these proverbs shows:

a) "A gossip goes about telling secrets, but one who is trustworthy in spirit keeps a confidence" (11.13).

b) "A wise child loves discipline, but a scoffer does not listen to rebuke" (13.1).

c) "Those who spare the rod hate their children, but those who love them are diligent to discipline them" (13.24).

d) "A faithful witness does not lie, but a false witness breathes out lies" (14.5).

e) "The simple believes everything, but the clever consider their steps. The wise are cautious and turn away from evil, but the fool throws off restraint and is careless" (14.15f.).

f) "Those who despise their neighbors are sinners, but happy are those who are kind to the poor" (14.21).

g) "The mind of the righteous ponders how to answer, but the mouth of the wicked pours out evil" (15.28).

h) "Those who ignore instruction despise themselves, but those who heed admonition will lodge with the wise" (15.32).

i) "Wealth brings many friends, but the poor are left friendless" (19.4).

j) "Discipline your children while there is hope; do not set your heart on their destruction" (19.18).

k) "Do not love sleep, or else you will come to poverty; open your eyes, and you will have plenty of bread" (20.13).

l) "Whoever says to the wicked, 'you are innocent,' will be cursed by peoples, abhorred by nations; but those who rebuke the wicked will have delight, and a good blessing will come upon them" (24.24f.).

"Do not say, 'I will do to others as they have done to me; I will pay them back for what they have done'" (24.29).

Chapter Twenty-Four

*Job's message was contrary to its
time's mainstream theology that
suffering was caused by sin alone.*

JOB

The book of Job is presented as a drama with a cast of characters that include Job, Satan, God, Job's three friends, and in a cameo, Job's wife. Satan challenges God and his faithful followers. Will Job remain loyal even if afflicted for no apparent reason?

Job is both victim and hero. He maintains that the tragedies in his life, the death of his children, the destruction of his property and his disease, are all undeserved. At the time, mainstream biblical ideology held that righteous people are rewarded while sinners are punished, so Job's friends argue that he must have sinned. That can be the only explanation for his suffering. This is what virtually every book of the Hebrew Bible maintains from Genesis 3 on. This position is clearly delineated in Deuteronomy.

The purpose of the book is to provide a suitable explanation for such a situation not only for Job, but for others. On the surface, Job appears to be unorthodox: it goes against mainstream teaching. In fact, when he is in the depths of extreme suffering, Job exhibits even greater faith. When his wife counsels him

"to curse God and die," he responds, "You speak as any foolish woman would speak. Shall we receive the good at the hand of God, and not receive the bad?" (2. 9-10)

He reinforces this assertion with:

"Naked I came from my mother's womb, and naked I shall return there; the Lord gave, and the Lord has taken away; blessed be the name of the Lord" (1. 21).

Human suffering is not necessarily deserved. Pain, sorrow, and distress may be unrelated to anything that humans have done, or failed to do. There is no way for people to understand fully the meaning of suffering. It is simply beyond human understanding. Job insisted on his right to question God:

"See, he will kill me; I have no hope; but I will defend my
ways to his face. This will be my salvation, that the godless
shall not come before him" (13. 15-16).

But God, speaking out of whirlwind, indicates his power and the inability
of humans to comprehend the mystery of God (38.1-42.6). Job again
asserts his faith: "For I know that my Redeemer lives, and that at the last
he will stand on the earth; after my skin has been thus destroyed, then in
my flesh I shall see God, whom I shall see on my side, and my eyes shall
behold, and not another. My heart faints within me!" (19. 25-27).

This fundamentally sacred book maintains that, regardless of what
happens to us, God is supreme. Without providing full answers to the deep
and painful experiences of human beings, Job has remained a source of
faith.

        If there is a secular element in this book of Job, it resides in
affirming the reality and power of God. God serves as the linchpin of
Israelite society, where, following the example of Job and his faith, they
may affirm their own faith regardless of any unfortunate circumstances
befalling their lives.

Chapter Twenty-Five

The Song of Songs is viewed as a
secular collection of sensual love
poems.

SONG OF SONGS

Ancient Israel was a society in which nature, fertility, and the life force were vital. So it's not surprising that physical love was of great interest. The poems which comprise the Song of Songs are sensual, sexual, and erotic. Physical passion was to be sought and experienced. In the text, it's attributed to Solomon, to legitimate its inclusion in the Hebrew Bible. Solomon was considered to be wise and a great lover, with 700 wives and 300 concubines.

The imagery of this collection of love poems is expressive and clear. As Akiba ben Joseph noted in the Second Century: Love, an essential element of human existence, is holy: "All the writings (of the Hebrew Bible) are holy but the Song of Songs is the Holy of Holies."

Many of his contemporaries and subsequent generations of Jews and Christians declined to accept this judgment. They chose to interpret the poems allegorically.

- Jews said that the love expressed was a reflection of God's relationship to Israel.
- Christians viewed it as illustrating God's love for the Church.
- Some believed that they were wedding songs.
- Others concluded that they comprised the liturgy of an ancient fertility cult.
- One scholar claims that it is comprised of thirty-one poems, a collection of love poems written by several poets, in different contexts;
- another scholar calls it a unity, and the composition of one author.

What is clear, however, is that the poems are thoroughly secular. They contain nothing of faith or other essential religious elements. God is not mentioned, neither are Israel nor its history. There's no intimation here of social concern or ethical consciousness.

The Song of Songs is a series of beautiful, sensual love poems which may be accepted as a joyful part of God's creation. Its holiness rests in its humanity and in the acceptance of sexual enjoyment as holy. It also reflects a mutuality in relationships between men and women, and between humans and the natural world. Men and women are treated in a non-sexist way, with women speaking as assertively as men and initiating romantic interludes as often as men. The following passages reflect the essence of this charming, thoroughly secular collection of poems.

Let him kiss me with the kisses of his mouth!
For your love is better than wine, your anointing oils are fragrant,
Your name is perfume poured out; therefore the maidens love you.
Draw me after you, let us make haste.
The king has brought me into his chambers.
We will exult and rejoice in you;
We will extol your love more than wine;
Rightly do they love you. **1.2-4**

I am a rose of Sharon, a lily of the valleys.
As a lily among brambles, so is my love among maidens.
As an apple tree among the trees of the wood,
So is my beloved among young men.
With great delight I sat in his shadow,
And his fruit was sweet to my taste.
He brought me to the banqueting house,
And his intention toward me was love. **2. 1-4**

Upon my bed at night I sought him whom my soul loves;
I sought him, but found him not;
I called him, but he gave no answer.
I will rise now and go about the city.
In the streets and in the squares;
I will seek him whom my soul loves.
I sought him, but found him not.
The sentinels found me, as they went about in the city.
Have you seen him whom my soul loves?
Scarcely had I passed them, when I found him whom my soul loves.
I held him, and would not let him go
Until I brought him into my mother's house,
And into the chamber of her that conceived me.

I adjure you, O daughters of Jerusalem,
By the gazelles or the wild does:
Do not stir up or awaken love until it is ready! **3.1-5**

Set me as a seal upon your heart, as a seal upon your arm;
For love is strong as death, passion fierce as the grave.
Its flashes are flashes of fire, a raging flame.
Many waters cannot quench love; neither can floods drown it.
If one offered for love all the wealth of his house,
it would be utterly scorned. **8.6-7**

LAMENTATIONS

The book of Lamentations includes five poems written in reaction to the destruction of Jerusalem in 586. Its central theme reflects the agony of the people, the apparent desertion of Zion by God and the hope that God will restore a humbled and repentant Israel. In this sense, it is a small Psalter.

Chapters 1, 2 and 4 contain dirges over the dead city;
Chapter 3 reflects the sadness of a desolate people,
and Chapter 5 contains liturgies recited at a time of national disaster.

These laments acknowledge the Israelites' guilt after being repeatedly warned by God for their idolatry. The power of God is acknowledged amid calls for his mercy.

This book is in the sacred mode, with God at its center.

Chapter Twenty-Seven

An anomalous book, Ecclesiastes, is described with references to its contrariness with Deuteronomy, its non-Judaean nature and later Talmudic controversy. It is a book of philosophy and resignation.

ECCLESIASTES (*Kohelet*)

Ecclesiastes, like Esther, is a thoroughly heterodox work. It is not concerned with the Hebrew Bible's usual issues. It contains nothing describing the special relationship of Israel with God, of the covenant, of the Temple, its rituals, and priesthood, or even some history of the people. It is a highly personal book, exploring the thoughts, questions, and conclusions of a person disturbed by life and its complexities, contradictions and frustrations.

The author clearly does not agree with the primary orientation found from Genesis-2 onward in the Hebrew Bible. Putting it simply, its orientation holds that God is the author of history and that the fate of peoples and individuals is determined by whether they obey, or do not obey, God's commandments. Retributive justice does not resonate for Ecclesiastes. Indeed, he is convinced that it is not an operative principle in life.

* In three of its chapters, God is not mentioned at all;

* in its other nine, references to God are sparse.

Strictly speaking, Ecclesiastes is not secular because God is present. Nevertheless God, as understood in the religious tradition of the Hebrew Bible, does not operate into human life -- at least as Ecclesiastes observes.

To proffer some indication of the deep dissonance between Ecclesiastes and most of the Hebrew Bible let us consider proof-texts, first from Deuteronomy:

➢ "Keep (God's) statutes and commandments, which I am commanding you today for your own well-being and that of your descendents after you, so that you may long remain in the land that the Lord your God is giving you for all time (Deut. 4.40).

> "Know therefore that the Lord your God is God, the faithful God who maintains covenant loyalty with those who love him and keep his commandments, to a thousand generations, and repays in their own person those who reject him" (Deut. 7.9f.).

> "See, I have set before you today life and prosperity, death and adversity. If you obey the commandments of the Lord your God, walking in his ways, and observing his commandments, decrees, and ordinances, then you will live and become numerous, and the Lord your God will bless you in the land you are entering to possess. But if your heart turns away and you do not hear, but are led astray to bow down to other gods and serve them, I declare to you today that you shall perish...choose life that you and your descendents may live, loving the Lord your God, and holding fast to him; for that means life to you and length of days..."(Deut. 30.15-20).

Now contrast these clear statements on the demands of God with the following statements from Ecclesiastes:

✓   "There is an evil that I have seen under the sun, and it lies heavy upon mankind: those to whom God gives wealth, possessions, and honor, so that they lack nothing of all they desire, yet God does not enable them to enjoy these things, but a stranger enjoys them. This is vanity; it is a grievous ill" (Ecc.6.1f.).

✓   "In my vain life I have seen everything; there are righteous people who perish in their righteousness, and there are wicked people who prolong their life in their evildoing. Do not be too righteous, and do not be too wise; why should you destroy yourself?" (Ecc.7.15f.).

✓   "All this I laid to heart, examining it all, how the righteous and the wise and their deeds are in the hand of God; whether it is love or hate one does not know. Everything that confronts them is vanity, since the same fate comes to all, to the righteous and the wicked, to the good and the evil, to the clean and the unclean, to those who sacrifice and those who do not sacrifice. As are those who are good, so are the sinners; those who swear are like those who shun the oath. This is an evil in all that happens under the sun, that is the same fate comes to everyone. Moreover, the hearts of all are full of evil; madness is in their hearts while they live, and after they go to the dead" (Ecc 9.1-3).

That Ecclesiastes was considered heterodox - or even heretical - is clear from an editor's claiming that it was the work of "the son of David, king in Jerusalem" (presumably, Solomon; 1.1).

Its last two verses:

> "The end of the matter; all has been heard. Fear God, and keep his commandments; for that is the whole duty of everyone. For God will bring every deed into judgment, including every secret thing, whether good or evil" (Ecc. 12.13f.).

legitimatize it further, and open a suspicion that they might have been added. That the editors of the Hebrew text realized that these verses were disharmonious with virtually all of the rest of the book is clear; these verses were scripted in lower case - probably by those who wanted to make it conform with mainstream Biblical ideology.

Moreover, the book's inclusion into the canon of the Hebrew Bible was debated toward the end of the first century CE[5]. In the Mishnah, compiled about 200 CE, we read the following:

"The Song of Songs renders the hands unclean.

- o Rabbi Judah says: 'The Song of Songs renders the hands unclean, but about Ecclesiastes there is dissension.'

- o Rabbi Jose says: 'Ecclesiastes does not render the hands unclean, and about the Song of Songs there is dissension.' Rabbi Simeon says: 'Ecclesiastes is one of things about which the School of Shammai adopted the more lenient, and the School of Hillel, the more stringent ruling.' (These are first century rabbis.)

- o "Rabbi Simeon ben Azzai said: 'I have heard a tradition from the seventy-two elders on the day they made Rabbi Eleazar ben Azariah head of the college (of Sages) that the Song of Songs and Ecclesiastes both render the hands unclean.' ...And if aught was in

---

[5] Elsewhere, BCE is denoted BC and CE is AD

dispute, dispute was about Ecclesiastes alone" (The Mishnah, Yadaim 3.5; Eduyot 5.3).

Despite this difference of opinion, Ecclesiastes made it into the Hebrew Bible. Just as the ideology of the Hebrew Bible was not uniform, neither were the opinions of first century rabbis.

In the Talmud, completed by the sixth century CE, the controversy continued.

o "Rab Judah son of Rabbi Samuel ben Shiath said in Rab's name: 'the Sages wished to hide the Book of Ecclesiastes because its words are self-contradictory; yet why did they not hide it? Because its beginning is religious teaching and its end is religious teaching...The Book of Proverbs too they tried to hide, because its statements are self-contradictory. Yet why did they not hide it?' They said: 'Did we not examine the Book of Ecclesiastes and find a reconciliation?'" (Talmud, Sabbath 30b).

The ancients decided that they were willing to live with what clearly was not mainstream ideology: Ecclesiastes became and remained a part of the canon.

Since there are no reliable historical references in the book, scholars, on analyzing the structure of its language, date it between 450 and 330. During Persia's domination of Judaea, its economic growth and trade were unprecedented. With economic advances also came volatility with the possibility of financial ruin. Many of Ecclesiastes' references indicate that situation.

"Sweet is the sleep of laborers whether they eat little or much; but the surfeit of the rich will not let them sleep. There is a grievous ill that I have seen under the sun: riches were kept by their owners to their hurt, and those riches were lost in a bad venture..."(5.12-14).

Envy and insecurity remained:

• "Then I saw that all toil and all skill in work come from one person's envy of another. This also is vanity and chasing after wind" (4.4).

- "Again I saw vanity under the sun: the case of solitary individuals, without sons or brothers; yet there is no end to all their toil, and their eyes are never satisfied with riches. 'For whom have I toiled' they ask, 'and depriving myself of pleasure?' This also is vanity and an unhappy business" (4.7f.).

- "The lover of money will not be satisfied with money; nor the lover of wealth, with gain. This also is vanity" (5.10).

- "I have seen slaves on horseback, and princes walking on foot like slaves" (10.7).

- "One can indeed come out of prison to reign, even though born poor in the kingdom" (4.14).

Just who Kohelet [Ecclesiastes] was is not known. He seems to have been a man of means, rather elderly and disenchanted with his life and his children. The word *kohelet* is the active feminine participle of the Hebrew word, *kahal*, which means gathering [synagogue also means gathering]. Perhaps the author was one who gathered knowledge and then students either formally or informally:

> "Besides being wise, the Teacher (Ecclesiastes) also taught people knowledge, weighing and studying and arranging many proverbs. The Teacher sought to find pleasing words, and he wrote words of truth plainly (12.9f.)."

Ecclesiastes is the Latinized form of the Greek translation of the Hebrew. Kohelet has also been called the Preacher after the Greek ecclesia (εκκλεσια), "assembly," or "church."

If the book of Ecclesiastes is famous for a single phrase, it is

> "Vanity of vanities, all is vanity" (1.2).

It appears thirty-eight times in the book and, in its way, that phrase summarizes Ecclesiastes' conclusions about human existence. That Hebrew word is '*hevel*': breath, vapor, something unsubstantial, hence, vain and futile. He writes of endless movement without progress:

"What has been is what will be, and there is nothing new under the sun...What is crooked cannot be made straight, and what is lacking cannot be counted" (1.9, 15). Even wisdom -- which he may have hoped would explain reality in a way which would give him hope -- has failed: "The wise have eyes in their head but fools walk in darkness. Yet I perceived the same fate befalls all of them. Then I said to myself, 'What happens to the fool will happen to me also; why then have I been so very wise?' And I said to myself that this also is vanity...There is nothing better for mortals than to eat and drink, and find enjoyment in their toil..."(2.14f., 24).

To Ecclesiastes, life seems fated to have been pre-determined, but why it happened as it did, and what it signifies is an impenetrable mystery.

❖ "For the fate of humans and the fate of animals is the same; as one dies, so does breath, and humans have no advantage over the animals; for all is vanity. All go to one place; all are from dust, and all turn to dust again...who can bring (them) to see what will be after them?" (3.19f., 22).

❖ "(God) has made everything suitable for its time; moreover he has put a sense of past and future into their minds, yet they cannot find out what God has done from the beginning to the end" (3.11).

❖ "And I thought the dead, who had already died, more fortunate than the living, who are still alive; but better than both is the one who has not yet been, and has not seen the evil deeds that are done under the sun" (4.2f.).

Ecclesiastes is haunted by the failure of wealth, family, wisdom, and success to satisfy him and to rescue him from the inevitability of death and blotting out of his existence.

"For there is no enduring remembrance of the wise or of fools, seeing that in the days to come all will have been long forgotten. How can the wise die just like fools? So I hated life, because what is done under the sun was grievous to me; for all is vanity and a chasing after wind" (2.16f.).

Ecclesiastes' values are secular. God is a reality for him but Ecclesiastes doesn't understand God's place in his life, nor does he find any satisfying answers. Still, as painful as those answers are to him, he does not shy away from them. He advises us that the facts of life must be faced, and that truth, as he understands it, should not be avoided. One must live with what cannot be changed, and accept the inevitable.

> "What is crooked cannot be made straight, and what is lacking cannot be counted" (1.15).

Even with life's uncertain capabilities, there is some enjoyment to be had in this life:

> "Go, eat your bread with enjoyment, and drink your wine with a merry heart; for God has long ago approved what you do. Let your garments always be white; do not let oil be lacking on your head. Enjoy life with the wife whom you love, all the days of your vain life that are given to you under the sun. Whatever your hand finds to do, do with all your might; for there is no work or thought or knowledge or wisdom in Sheol (the netherworld) to which you are going" (9.7-10).

While God is a reality for Ecclesiastes, he denies what is stressed in most of the Hebrew Bible. Here, God is inscrutable and mysterious. The God who revealed himself and his will through Moses and his chosen people is unknown to Ecclesiastes. Reason is the only way to knowledge for him. Humans cannot change the world and all efforts to this end are vain.

In the place of a religion of faith, hope and obedience, Ecclesiastes offers a philosophy of resignation and a mood of disillusionment. His ethics are secular, having no relationship to divine commandments. They arise out of necessity. To him, life is for the most part inexplicable so one must accept what is fated and cannot be changed.

Ecclesiastes is a fascinating combination of the rationalist agnostic, the skeptic, the pessimist and fatalist. It is amazing that this book was made a part of the Hebrew Bible - demonstrating the glory of this great work.

DANIEL

Scholarly consensus holds that the book of Daniel is the latest composition of the Hebrew Bible, possibly completed in 164 during the Hasmonean dynasty. But it is set back in the sixth century under the reigns of powerful Babylonian and Persian kings.

Daniel is portrayed as the model of Jewish faithfulness to God. The first six chapters depict him as a member of Babylon's Jewish exile community. He rises to a position of importance as a court official, one dealing with the issues of Jews living under a foreign king. Daniel's experiences are reminiscent of the stories of Joseph (in Genesis) and Esther; both of them held high court positions outside the land of Israel. Unlike them, however, Daniel was totally loyal to God, while the Joseph and Esther accounts are essentially secular.

The second half of Daniel contains a series of apocalyptic visions, which reveal a cataclysmic result and a transformation of history. In the end, God and Israel triumph.

While the two sections are entirely different in content, they share some common themes:
* ❖ God's sovereignty over history and foreign monarchs,
* ❖ Devotees of God have special wisdom and insight.

They present an ideal of heroic obedience to God, even to the point of death.

Unlike Esther and her uncle, Mordecai, who save their fellow Jews through their own human efforts, Daniel constantly turns to God and remains loyal to him and his demands even as his life is threatened.

Against court practice, Daniel refuses to eat food prohibited by Biblical law and remains healthy (1:8-15).

* He refuses to bow down to King Nebuchadnezzar, is thrown into the fiery furnace, and survives (3:1-29).

Court officials envious of Daniel's success have King Darius issue a decree forbidding worship of any divinity or human except the king.

Anyone who does so will be thrown into a lion's den. Daniel perseveres in praying to God three times each day as he had always done. Thrown to the lions, he was rescued by an angel of God – and his accusers were then thrown to the lions (6:1-24).

In this totally sacred book, God's power is limitless, and that is acknowledged not only by Daniel, but also by foreign kings as well.

> "The king, Nebuchadnezzar, said to Daniel: 'Truly, your god is the God of gods and Lord of kings and a revealer of mysteries, for you have been able to reveal this mystery'" (2:47).

> "I (Darius) make a decree that in all my royal dominion people should tremble and fear before the God of Daniel, for he is the living God, enduring forever. His kingdom shall never be destroyed, and his dominion has no end. He delivers and rescues…" (6:26f.).

The book's secular purpose is to encourage Jews of the diaspora to maintain their identity and loyalty to God, who will care for them like he did for Daniel. Even powerful foreign kings believed in God! The book concludes with the promise of a felicitous end:

"Happy are those who persevere and attain the thousand three hundred thirty-five days. But you, go your way, and rest; you shall rise for your reward at the end of days" (12:12-13).

Chapter Twenty-Nine

*The drama of Esther, the heroine, celebrated
by the ancient Feast of Lots (Purim)*

ESTHER

The 2nd century Book of Esther is a drama in six acts. It along with Song
of Songs is unique in the Hebrew Bible, for there is no mention of God in
either.

Esther opens with the king of Persia, Ahasuerus (generally identified as
Khshayarsha commonly called Xerxes I, 486-465), giving a lavish banquet
for his nobles lasting 180 days, followed by a seven day banquet for all his
subjects living in the capital, Susa. While the guests were well-intoxicated,
the king summoned his queen, Vashti,
   "wearing a royal diadem, to display her beauty..." (1.1-5, 8-12).
The queen refused. Some commentaries suggest that she was asked to
appear in the nude Fearing that her refusal would set a bad precedent and
example, Vashti was banished from the court and the quest
   "for another who is more worthy than she" (1.17-19)
was initiated Of the many young virgins who were presented to the king, a
young Jewess, Esther, was selected (2.8f.). Esther was an orphan who had
been adopted by her cousin, Mordecai.
   Some time later, while Mordecai was sitting at the palace gate, he
learned that two of the king's eunuchs were plotting to assassinate the
king. Mordecai told Queen Esther who reported it to the king, who then
had the eunuchs executed. The event was then recorded in the royal annals
(2.21-23).

In addition to Esther, Mordecai, and the king, there is a fourth major actor
in this drama: Haman, an Agagite. The king promoted him above all of his
other officials. All who met Haman bowed down to him, except for
Mordecai. No reason is given for this, but it may relate to the experience
of the Jews with the Agagites: Agag was the foe of King Saul who
indirectly cost him his kingdom (I Samuel 15.8-33). More importantly
Agag was the king of Amelek, the archetypal enemy of Israel (Exodus
17.14-17; Deut. 25.17-19). No knowledgeable Jew would bow down to a
person with that background.

In anger, Haman plotted to kill not only Mordecai, but all the Jews in the kingdom (3.1-6). Haman then went to the king, and defamed the Jews as different from other people, since they did not obey the king's laws. The king then issued a decree to carry out Haman's plot (3.7-12).

Mordecai after reading a copy of the decree delivered to Esther, asked her to go to the king and plead with him on behalf of her people. Esther hesitated, since no one was allowed to approach the king without being summoned. Mordecai warned her that neither she nor her family would be spared, if she did not intervene, so she agreed (4.1-17).

An interlude leads to the conclusion of the drama: Unable to sleep, the king requests royal records and discovers that it was Mordecai who saved him from assassins, but he had never been rewarded. The king summoned Haman to honor and reward Mordecai. Haman grew concerned for himself and his plot (6.1-14).

The king and Haman were guests at a feast which Esther gave. She then revealed Haman's plan to the king. In fury, the king left the banquet hall; Haman joined Esther on her couch and implored her for his life. When the king returned and saw them together on the couch, he cried out:

"Does he mean to ravish the queen in my own palace?" (7.1-10).

The king had Haman executed on the very stake he had put up for Mordecai. The king then issued a new decree reversing Haman's edict to kill all the Jews. The Jews were saved by the actions of Mordecai and Esther and many non-Jewish Persians converted to Judaism (8.7-10, 17).

The Book of Esther is a thoroughly secular novella. There is no mention of God in it. Many commentators see God in the following sentence:

"For if you persist in keeping silent at a time like this, relief
and deliverance will appear for the Jews from another quarter;
but you and your family will perish. It's possible that you
came to the throne for just such a moment as this" (4.14).

This is what Mordecai told his cousin and adopted daughter, Esther, as he asks her to intercede with the king of Persia.

The phrase, "from another quarter," is widely thought to refer to God. Those who hold to this interpretation cannot accept the fact that a book in the Hebrew Bible lacks any reference to God, or that Jewish people in crisis might not turn to God. It is certainly true that throughout the Hebrew Bible, Israelites turned to God when in dire straits. They did it over and over again when attacked by their neighbors. As recorded in the

Book of Judges: God would send a Judge, a charismatic military leader, to rescue them. It is also clear in the Psalms, where the poets repeat God's role as savior and comforter.

God's absence in the Book of Esther is just what makes it a revolutionary work within the Hebrew Bible. "From another quarter" within the context of Esther implies that: if Esther didn't carry out her mission, another human would do so.

The Book of Esther reveals nothing of faith or other essential religious elements one might expect within a book of the Hebrew Bible. Not only is God not mentioned but no mention is made of the mighty acts of God throughout biblical history nor are its usual themes and concepts given space : there is nothing at all about the covenant, prayer, circumcision, kashrut (food laws), Sabbath observance, the Temple in Jerusalem, sacrifices, or biblical law.

The Jews were saved through Esther's fortunate social position and courage, as well as Mordecai having saved the king's life, and through his wise counsel. Jews survived not through faith in God or his intervention, but through the efforts of Jews who did not turn to God for help.

The Book of Esther, while positively Jewish, is thoroughly secular. The Book of Daniel offers a contrast. Daniel is also a Diaspora Jew[6], living in the time of Nebuchadnezzar and the Persian king, Darius. While Esther and Mordecai are thoroughly acculturated into Persian society, exhibiting no special Jewish practices, Daniel and his two friends observe kashrut, pray only to Yahweh, and maintain their religious loyalty even at the risk of death. They are rescued by God from both a fiery furnace and a lion's den. So wondrous were these events that the king affirmed God's power (Daniel 2.47f; 3.28) (6.26f.).

Daniel was open about his Jewish identity, and about practicing his religion. The opposite was the case with Esther, who was advised by Mordecai to keep her identity secret:

> "Esther did not reveal her people or kindred, for Mordecai had
> told her not to reveal it (2.10)."

Their names tell us how fully-acculturated they were: Mordecai is named for Marduk (Merodach), the chief god in the Babylonian pantheon, while Esther is named for Ishtar, the chief female deity in the Assyrian and Babylonian pantheon.

---

[6] One living outside the land of Israel.

The heroes of these two books seem to follow the advice of the prophet Jeremiah, given to the Judaeans who were exiled to Babylonia after the destruction of the Temple in Jerusalem in 586. He counseled them to live full lives there, and went so far as to have them

> "seek the welfare of the city where I (God) have sent you into exile, and pray to the Lord on its behalf, for in its welfare you will find your welfare" (Jeremiah 29.4-7).

Clearly, Jews of the far-flung Diaspora followed widely divergent paths in exhibiting their special identity.

That some Jews in antiquity were upset by the secular nature of Esther is clear in those additions to Esther found in the Septuagint[7] which come down to us only in Greek. These additions are also found in the Apocrypha; they attempt to rectify what the authors felt was lacking in the Hebrew Bible's version. The name of God or Lord appears over fifty times. Esther is seen as having antipathy toward intermarriage while in the Hebrew Bible Mordecai indicates that Esther's fate – her marriage to King Ahasuerus -- was what would save the Jews of Persia. Interpolations abound: "fear God and keep his commandments" (2.10/HB; 2.20 Apoc.); "call upon the Lord" (4.8 both);

> "that night the Lord took sleep from the king" (6.1 both).

The Greek version has many additions, many omissions and, in contrast with the Hebrew Bible, several explicitly religious concerns.

Esther is the only book of the Hebrew Bible that the Dead Sea sect at Qumran did not copy. If they had, maybe another ancient insight might have been given us about Jewish thought.

Given the pressures to assimilate, life in the Jewish Diaspora was always problematic. Some of these pressures were for social and material success, as well as withstanding periodic episodes of virulent anti-Jewish sentiment and action. Just as conditions varied from place to place and from time-to-time, so did the Jewish arsenal of adaptations and defenses contain various strategies. Daniel followed the established path of the of the Hebrew Bible in putting God at the center of concern for meaning and security. Esther and Mordecai followed a secular approach, using guile and service.

---

[7] The Greek translation of the Hebrew Bible.

Chapter Thirty

This is the four-stage story of the
return of exiles to rebuild the
Temple and reinstitution of God as
central to Judaism's survival.

EZRA-NEHEMIAH

The books of Ezra and Nehemiah include a variety of materials covering the return of some exiles to Jerusalem.

It takes place after the 538 conquest of Babylonia by Cyrus the Great. This return led to the reestablishment of the Judaean community centered in Jerusalem. Accompanying their return was the rebuilding of their destroyed Temple, along with completing the wall around the city. Ezra and Nehemiah provisioned the future path of the Jewish people by developing techniques for their survival.

What they did is presented as a fulfillment of the prophecies of the prophets, and as a continuation of Jewish history going back to its beginnings. Of particular significance are the prophecies of Jeremiah and of Isaiah-of-the-Exile. They provided the basic ideologies for survival after the debacle of the Babylonian conquest with their exiling most of Judaea's populace.

Jeremiah suggested that the people could maintain their cohesiveness without the Temple and the sacrificial cult. He also instructed them to accommodate themselves to the exile: to settle in, marry and have children, plant trees and farm; and to cooperate peaceably with their host society for their own benefit. He promised that, at some time in the not-too-distant future, they would return to their homeland. That they prospered in Babylonia and then Persia is clear. Some of them achieved positions in the royal court. They, while still living in Persia, supported those who returned.

Isaiah's message concerning God's choosing them for a special mission, provided the motivation for its continuity. He further explained that their suffering had been for a higher purpose. His messianic vision gave them the hope that things would improve. His exalted view of God's power also promised that all of this could be realized. Their condition in exile was apparently good, and many of them returned to Judaea, where the situation gradually became secure.

The society, which developed under the leadership of those who returned from exile, was a fully sacralized one. It was centered around the Temple and led by a restored priesthood and the sacrificial cult. But it was secular in that humans achieved it with God, for the most part, relegated to the background. Although they are not secular as in Esther, where God is not even mentioned, God's presence is only cursory in Ezra/Nehemiah. In them he only sets the stage for what is to occur, rather than initiating and carrying out events.

This is unlike God's active role as portrayed in the Pentateuch and the histories. This change in emphasis is shown in Nehemiah (Neh. 9.1-37). Nehemiah is portrayed as the force in charge of the events he carried out (6.6-9, 15-16). Judaean leaders could have carried out their programs only with the acquiescence and cooperation of the Persian kings (Ezra 1.1-4; 6.3-12; Nehemiah 1.11-2.10).

Support for the returnees came not only from the Persian monarchy but also from those Judaeans who did not return from exile. Apparently they were satisfied with their lives, and were willing to support the returnees with material to rebuild Judaea (Ezra 1.5-6).

That is how began the widespread custom of Jews in the Diaspora maintaining a strong and helping relationship with their homeland. The reality for the returnees was that they would no longer be politically independent; their survival was based on their becoming a socio-religious community. They attempted to preserve their identity by self-segregation from their non-Jewish neighbors.

These books cover four stages, from Cyrus (538) through the reign of Artaxerxes II (358).

1) The first stage begins with Sheshbazzar, a Jewish court official, sent to Jerusalem to rebuild the Temple. He came with the treasure of the Temple taken by Nebuchadnezzar, (Ezra 1.7- 11).
2) Zerubbabel and Jeshua, who restored the sacrifices on the site of the Temple, led the second stage. The Temple, over the opposition of some of the non-Jewish populace, was completed later. (Ezra 5.1-6.22). With this accomplishment and the presence of the

priesthood, a hierocracy, rule by the priesthood was established. While much was needed be done to secure the community, the basic structure was now in place.

3) The third stage brought Ezra and another contingent to Judaea. He too, had been appointed by the king (Ezra 7.11-26). Ezra's major accomplishment was reestablishing the Mosaic code, which he personally presented to the people (Nehemiah 7.72-8.12). This would serve as their constitution.

4) Another court official sent from Babylon led the fourth and final stage: Nehemiah, the king's cup-bearer. He secured Jerusalem by rebuilding its walls, and by establishing the milieu for the purity of the community and its worship (Neh. 1.1-7.72). Nehemiah's role in securing the emerging community was essentially secular, as he settled disputes between his fellow Judaeans and the non-Jewish population.

A key tactic of both Ezra and Nehemiah was to separate the Jews from the non-Jewish population. Non-Jews were comprised both by those who lived in the area prior to 586, and those whom the conquerors brought in to replace exiled-Judaeans. The latter group was not allowed to share in the rebuilding program, or to have any role in governing the community.

The returnees also attempted to separate them further by legislating against intermarriage, and to separate those who had married. There was an apparent fear that the Jews would be demographically swamped with their special identity either being severely diluted, or even obliterated.

To prevent this, they sought to establish an endogamous nation with marriage permitted only within the Jewish nation (Ezra 9.1-15; 10.1-44; Nehemiah 10.28-30; 13.1-3, 23-27). Given intermarriage's apparent extent, this was unrealistic. Among those especially mentioned as prohibited from marrying were Moabites and Ammonites. The book of Ruth may have been written, in part, to counter this attitude: after all, she was the great-grandmother of David and a Moabite. (Ruth 4.16-17).

Just as God gave the Torah to Moses on Mt. Sinai, Ezra presented the Torah to the Judaeans in a restored Jerusalem. Humans were now responsible for the fate of their people. While the community was to be a sacralized one, its leadership responded to concrete communal needs, with

God in the background. Persia allowed Judaean society a modicum of independence; a society led by priests would be no military threat to them.

> The process described in the books of Ezra and Nehemiah became the practice of Jews from then on, with the brief second-century exception of the Hasmoneans who enjoyed eighty years of political independence. After the Greeks [in 333] and Romans [in 68] ended that dynasty, the priest-led situation resumed.

It was not until 1948 that another Jewish state was founded.

Chapter Thirty-One

*Ruth is presaged and promoted as
the model for intermarriage and
diversity for the survival of Jewish
Identity.*

RUTH

The book of RUTH provides a fascinating follow-up to Ezra and
Nehemiah.

Ezra and Nehemiah had prohibited mixed marriages, particularly those
with Moabites and Ammonites. They were denigrated because of the story
of their having come into existence when after fleeing the destruction of
Sodom and Gomorrah, the daughters of Lot had sex with him. (Genesis
19.36-38.

Israelites were specifically prohibited from marrying them:

> "No Ammonite or Moabite shall be admitted into the
> congregation of the Lord; none of their descendants, even to
> the tenth generation, shall ever be admitted into the
> congregation of the Lord..." (Deut. 23. 4-5).

When some Israelites "profaned themselves by whoring with Moabite
women and worshiped their god, Baal-peor...they were to be publicly
slain" (Numbers 25.1-5).

In spite of all this, the heroine of this book is a Moabite woman,
Ruth. She is portrayed as loyal and loving toward her mother-in-law,
Naomi. After her husband and sons died, Naomi planned to return to Israel
from Moab and told her two widowed daughters-in-law to remain with
their people. While one agreed, Ruth was determined to remain with her
mother-in-law and spoke her most famous words:

> "Do not urge me to leave you, to turn back and not follow you.
> For wherever you go, I will go; wherever you lodge, I will
> lodge; your people shall be my people, and your God my
> God" (Ruth 1.16).

Nothing negative is stated or suggested regarding Moabites or Ruth. This Moabite had high status; she was the great grandmother of David, and is placed alongside Rachel and Leah in the sparse ranks of famous Biblical women (4.16-17; 11-12).

In its narration, the general absence of God makes clear the secular nature of this book. The only action attributed to God is,

"The Lord let her (Ruth) conceive" (4.13).

In spite of the strictures against intermarriage in Ezra and Nehemiah and elsewhere in the Hebrew Bible, the reality was that the mixed population among whom the Judaeans lived made necessary accepting some intermarriages.

Ruth becomes a balance to the harshness of those who would not only prohibit such alliances, but would also attempt to break them up. After all, many special Israelites married those from other groups:

- ✓ Abraham fathered Ishmael from his Egyptian concubine, Hagar (Gen. 6.3).

- ✓ Moses was married to Zipporah, the daughter of a Midianite priest, Jethro (Exodus 2.21).

- ✓ Joseph married Asenath, an Egyptian (Gen. 41.45).

- ✓ Solomon married Ammonites and Moabites, among many others from various places, including Egypt (1 Kings 11.1).

The book of Ruth is a model for the diversity of ideas and practices in Biblical society. While those directing society may have had definite and narrow concepts, the culture found space for divergence. It may be postulated, in the interests of the survival of the people.

Chapter Thirty-Two

Chronicles I and II are reiterations
of Samuel and Kings to promote a
sacred cult.

CHRONICLES

The two volumes of Chronicles are essentially one book.

What is termed Chronicles I details genealogies from Adam to the exiles in Babylonia in its first nine chapters; its next twenty chapters recapitulate the reign of David.

The second book covers the period from Solomon to the conquest of Jerusalem, the exile to Babylonia and the decree of Cyrus, which allowed the exiles to return to Judaea. Most of the material is selectively drawn from 1 Samuel 31-2 Kings 25, with additional material from unknown sources.

Chronicles is fundamentally a sacred account of the monarchy. Its new perspectives and meanings were developed for the new religio-political reality arising during the second Temple period. The monarchy had been destroyed, so now Israel's reason for survival rested in the Temple cult and its priesthood. Chronicles provides the foundation for the importance of the restored Temple -- and for the necessity of supporting the priesthood.

The Davidic dynasty is glorified and expanded, while the other kings – Saul and the monarchs of the ten northern tribes – are delegitimized. It is possible that David is featured because he proposed the building of the first Temple, and may have been seen as a link to a future saving king, the messiah.

This book offers a unique view of God's compassion and grace as survival's operative principle, offering eternal hope. The bond between God and the true Israel is reflected in the sacrality of those times. It reveals a divinely empowered kingdom with God at its center, in a sacred place: the Temple.

Chapter Thirty-Three
*The author postulates the four-step
process from polytheism to
Monotheism*

THE GOD CONCEPT
Achieving A Secular Goal Through A Sacred Process
The reality of God is central to the ideology of the Bible. God is seen as the Creator, and the Author of History. He is held to be unique and solitary, there being no other god. This is made clear in Genesis 1 where God's power is manifest, and His existence taken for granted. Only fools would not recognize this as fact (Jeremiah 4.22). With creation a certainty, a creator was viewed as a necessity. The Israelites believed this; there was no discussion or debate about it. Similarly Abraham, the first Hebrew, held that there was a single God to whom one's essential relationship was to be obedience (Genesis 12.1,4; 22.1-2,10).

The reality of Biblical society was quite contrary to its belief doctrine. From the time of the Patriarchs, Abraham, Isaac, and Jacob, the Israelites worshipped many gods. This practice continued until the sacking of Jerusalem and the destruction of the first Temple by the Babylonians in 586. The Biblical text testifies to this through its historical and prophetic books. It is possible that Abraham, Moses and others were monotheists, but that most of the population had absorbed the polytheism of the Canaanites and others.

ISRAELITE POLYTHEISM or IDOLATRY
Another possibility - one held in this study - is that the Israelites were polytheists who gradually evolved into monolatry (acceptance of other gods but ours is supreme) and finally adopted monotheism, but only some 250 years after it was first conceptualized, possibly by the prophet Amos (ca. 740).

The basic proof text - only one of many - is
"who is like you, O Lord (Yahweh) among the (other) gods?"
(Exodus 15.11).
That the Biblical authors acknowledged that Israelites engaged in polytheism is clear in Aaron's ready response to the demand of the people for gods (elohim) "who would go before us" (Ex. 32.1).

While the Pentateuch does not deal with historical times, the various traditions that developed it were aware that idolatry was pervasive in the period before Joshua's conquest of Canaan, and the existence of the gods of other nations was accepted; this is made clear from:

> "and against all the gods of Egypt, I the Lord will exact judgments" (Ex. 12.12).
> "You shall have no other gods before Me" (Ex 20.3).
> "You shall not inquire of their gods" (Deut. 12.30).
> "For they also burn their sons and daughters in fire to their gods" (Josh. 22.22).
> "You shall not remember the name of their gods" (Josh. 23.7).

It may be argued that the "historical" accounts, albeit in heavily edited texts, begin with the book of Judges. In it is a repetition of lapses into idolatry by the tribes. Those lapses inevitably led to the tribe being conquered by their neighbors. The Deuteronomists of the Sixth Century see those political losses as consequences for idolatry. Such idolatry is reflected by a text showing that Jewish society was then thoroughly acculturated into the cults of Canaan.

This is made clear in the Gideon/Jerubbaal narrative (Judges 6-8). The name, Jerubbaal, "he who strives for Baal" (6.31) indicates his attachment to Baal who was one of the major gods of Canaan. His father, Joash, had erected an altar to Baal and Asherah, a Canaanite goddess. While Gideon was challenged by the populace for destroying the altar of Baal and Asherah, his subsequent actions indicate that he also was an idolater - and his action against Baal was added during the reworking of the text. He called upon the populace to contribute golden earrings, crescents, pendants, and chains that he made into an ephod, a priestly garment (8.24-26).

The book of Judges had at least two purposes. The Gideon story contains both points of view.:

1. a protest against idolatry (reflecting a later period). The "conservatives," those who wished to maintain the existing political situation, were anti-monarchical. When Gideon was offered the kingship, he refused: "I will not rule over you and my son shall not rule over you. The Lord will rule over you" (8.22f.). This reflects the opposition to a monarchy by the traditional elites

and possibly the priests. This is also reflected in Samuel's later opposition to the establishment of a monarchy (1 Samuel 8.1-22);

2. the argument for and against a dynastic monarchy which would provide greater military security for the tribes.   Judges also includes pro-monarchical sentiments which are summarized in the last verse of the book: "In those days, there was no king in Israel; every man did what was right in his own eyes" (which was wrong!) (21.25). Included in what was wrong was the repeated, constant idolatry and various severe moral failures such as the "outrage" at Gibeah (19-21).

BIBLICAL EXAMPLES OF IDOLATRY

The most dramatic display of pervasive idolatry is reflected in the story of Micaiah (17-18). He used his mother's funds to fashion a graven and molten image as well as an ephod and teraphim bearing the images of heathen deities. The formula found in the last verse of the book is repeated here (17.6) as well as at the beginning of the "outrage" narrative (19.1). Indicative of the acceptance of idolatry, Micaiah hired a "levite" as his priest to minister in his chapel of idols. At this time "levites" were probably members of a priestly guild, rather that members of the priestly tribe of Levi. Micaiah's priest was not a Levite but a "levi," *one attached to gods*. He was denoted as a 'lad from Bethlehem of Judaea, from the family of Judah' (17.7).

That idolatry was the norm is made even clearer with the arrival of spies of the tribe of Dan to Micaiah's property. After ignoring the protests of the levite, they took him and the idols stating,

"…is it better for you to be a priest to one man or to be a priest
to a tribe and a family in Israel?" (18.19).

They then transported the priest and the idols with them and established them in their new home in Laish which they renamed as Dan.

Even more outrageous was their appointing Jonathan, the son of Gershom, and the grandson of Moses, as well as Jonathan's sons to be priests of their idolatrous sanctuary

"until the captivity of the land," in 586 (18.30f.).

. (The Hebrew text indicates that later editors did not wish to associate Moses with such activities. Because of this, the equivalent of an 'N' was added to the letters: M(o)^{N}Sheh, identifying the priest as Manasseh).

David is also associated with idolatry. When David had to flee from Saul, his wife, Michal,

> "took the teraphim and placed it on the bed...and covered it, stating that it was David" (1 Sam. 19.13).

Sometime later, when

> "David danced before the Lord... (he) was girded with a linen ephod" (II Sam. 6.14).

That the ephod (used as a cult article) was linked to the teraphim and idolatry is clear in Judges 17-18 and Hosea 3.4. When David was defending himself with Saul, he stated that if his bad relations with Saul were the result of other men, they should be "cursed before the Lord because they have driven me away this day from joining myself with the inheritance of the Lord, saying, 'go, serve other gods'" (1 Sam. 26.19).

Solomon was lionized for his wisdom, his building of the Temple, and his peaceful reign. However, he, too, was deeply involved in idolatry. His kingdom was to be split because he went after

> "other gods" (I Kings 11.10f.).

The fault, according to Biblical historians, rested with his many foreign wives "who turned his heart after other gods" (I King 11.2).

That Israelite society was idolatrous is also clearly seen in the action of Jeroboam, the king of the Ten Northern Tribes (Israel). Following Solomon's death, the northern part of the kingdom appealed to his son, Rehoboam, for relief from the high taxes Solomon had instituted. They felt that they were unfairly taxed for the benefit of Judaea. When their appeal was rejected, they separated and installed Jeroboam as their king. One of his first acts was to install images of golden calves at Bethel in the south and at Dan in the north (I Kings 12.26-33).

The political importance of the Jerusalem cult is made clear in these words of Jeroboam,

> "You have gone up long enough to Jerusalem. Behold, (these) are your gods, Israel, who brought you up from the land of Egypt" (I Kings 12.28).

Political and cultic unity were understood as mutually reinforcing of group identity.

MONOLATRY

The first historical person to develop a concept of a single God who ruled over all seems to have been Amos, the 8th Century prophet. In the first two chapters of the book of Amos, God is clearly seen as the God of all nations. His concept of God includes seeing God demanding ethical behavior in relationships among people. His idea of God is reflected in the pronouncements of several other prophets, particularly Michah, Isaiah and Jeremiah. Throughout subsequent history, it is clear that: Amos' insights were not broadly accepted until the 586 conquest of Judaea by Babylonia and its destruction of the first Temple.

IDOLATRY

The last decades of the Judaean monarchy were permeated with idolatry and polytheism. During the reign of Hezekiah (715-687):

> "he suppressed the hill-shrines, smashed the sacred pillars...broke up the bronze serpent that Moses had made; for up to that time the Israelites had been burning sacrifices to it" (2 Kings 18.4).

During the reign of Manasseh (687-642):

> "He did what was wrong in the eyes of the Lord, in following the abominable practices of the nations...He rebuilt the hill-shrines which his father Hezekiah had destroyed and erected altars to Baal...he built altars for all the host of heaven and worshipped them in the two courts of the house of the Lord. He made his son pass through fire, he practiced sooth-saying and divination and dealt with ghosts and spirits...the image of the goddess Asherah he put in the house of the (Lord)..." (2 Kings 21.2-7).

During the reign of Josiah (640-609):

> "...the king ordered Hilkiah, the high priest...to remove from the house of the Lord all the objects made for Baal and Asherah and all the host of heaven...he suppressed the heathen priests whom the kings of Judaea had appointed to burn sacrifices at the hill-shrines...as well as those who burnt sacrifices to Baal, to the sun and moon and planets and all the host of heaven...He also pulled down the houses of the male prostitutes attached to the house of the Lord, where the women wove vestments in honor of Asherah...He desecrated

Tophes...so that no one might make his son or daughter pass through fire in honor of Molech...he burnt the chariots of the sun..." (2 Kings 23.4-7, 10-11).

The pervasiveness of idolatry in all levels of society is seen in this passage in Jeremiah about Judaeans who settled in Egypt after 586:

"Then all the men who knew that their wives were burning sacrifices to other gods and the crowds of women standing by answered Jeremiah, 'We will not listen to what you tell us in the name of the Lord. We intend to fulfill all the promises by which we have bound ourselves: we will burn sacrifices to the queen of heaven and pour drink-offerings to her as we used to do, we and our fathers, our kings and our princes, in the cities of Judaea and in the streets of Jerusalem'" (Jeremiah 44.15-17).

MONOTHEISM

The seeds of monotheism had been first planted by Amos and were harvested by Isaiah of the Exile (after 586) when he stated:

"...I am God, there is no one like me" (Isaiah 46.9).

The process of moving from polytheism and idolatry - including worshipping one's national God (monolatry) - to monotheism took many centuries. Ideologues – prophets – conceptualized this idea of God, but it gradually worked its way only through the general population as is clear from Biblical text. Once developed, monotheism was read back in time, to the first creation story (Genesis 1) and to the first Hebrew, Abraham (Genesis 12).

THE NAME OF GOD

This process is also exemplified in the names given to God.

אלהים

One of the two major names, Elohim, (אלהים) literally means "gods." It is used overwhelmingly in the Hebrew text to mean God, but occasionally means "gods," "chieftains," and "judges."

אל

El, the singular form, was the name of the aged and kingly patriarch of the Canaanite pantheon. Possibly because of the Israelite adoption of the name for God, there are no polemics against El (אל), only against Baal, the young storm god and divine warrior of the Canaanite pantheon. Just what mental process led the Israelites to adopt a plural noun for their single, unique God is unknown. Possibly it was to distinguish their God, Elohim, from the Canaanite, El. Or, possibly, they conceived that their God (the plural Elohim) had the powers normally attributed to their other gods, including El.

יהוה

The other major name of God in the Bible is generally pronounced Yahweh (יהוה). As it stands, it has no literal meaning. It denotes what had originated as the national deity of the Israelites, later seen as the single deity of the universe. Yahweh is also known as Elohim. However, the meaning of Yahweh is not very mysterious and the Bible makes its origin and meaning clear. The Hebrew consonants which comprise Yahweh are: י (yod), ה (hay), ו (vav), ה (hey). As noted, in this form, it has no exact meaning, although scholars have proposed numerous grammatical constructions and transitions. By changing one letter, the ו vav to a י yod, we have, (יהיה yi-hi-yeh), "he will be." A clue to this is found in Exodus 3.13f.: Moses asks God what his name is: "God answered:

" I will be what I will be."

The Hebrew is "eh-heh-yeh ah-sher eh-he-yeh." "Eh-heh-yeh" is the first person singular future (imperfect in Hebrew grammar). "Y-hi-yeh" is the third person singular future, "he will be."

'Whoever' developed these two names for God seems to have sought to give Israel's God a unique name, one totally unknown in the ancient world. He also wanted to communicate the ideal of absolute power and freedom to God, as implied in the Exodus passage:

"I God will be and do whatever I God deem correct regardless
of what any humans desire or believe ought to be done."

The blending of the two major names for God is testified to in this passage in Joshua:

"God (el), God (elohim), the Lord (Yahweh), God (el), God
(elohim), the Lord (Yahweh), He knows" (22.22).

אל שדי

According to the Bible, a third name for God, the only one known to the patriarchs, was ale shaddai (אל שדי):

"and I appeared to Abraham, to Isaac, to Jacob as ale shaddai
but (by) name, Yahweh, I was not known to them" (Exodus
6.2).

Ale shaddai is usually translated as "God Almighty." Other suggestions
have also been proposed. Until recently, the obvious translation "God of
my breasts" was not proposed. El, of course, in one of the common names
for god/God and shaddai (my breasts) appears in various places in the
Bible, particularly in the Song of Songs. That shaddai should be translated
as "my breasts" is attested to by a passage in Genesis:

"From the God (El) of your father – so may he help you. By
(El/God) of my breasts (Shaddai) – so may he bless you…the
blessings of breast(s) (shaddaim) and womb" (49.25).

This name seems to be related to a goddess cult. If so, it did not and could
not endure in the developing monotheism of Israel.

Ideology is developed to explain reality, to provide meaning in life, and to
move society in a given direction. Conceptions of deities grow out of
specific contexts. Gods and goddesses reveal the needs and aspirations of
those who adhered to them. Basic to every society is the requirement for
sustenance. A major aspect of every religious system, therefore, was the
promotion of fertility. Some form of father-mother-child gods reflecting
the cycle of procreation was worshipped and offered sacrifices, both
propitiatory and in thanksgiving. Other deities represented elements of
nature or modes of human behavior such as love and conflict. The
recognition of the reality of death, in some societies, led to systems
insuring immortality.

Israelite society, as is clear from the Biblical text, was polytheistic
until the destruction of the first Temple. The cults of Canaan as well as
those of Egypt and Mesopotamia influenced it. A dramatic ideological
innovation developed through the insight of individuals who sought an
explanation for the special condition of Israel: a small, generally
beleaguered nation, totally lacking in unity.

One may view the development of monotheism as the last gasp of a
helpless, tiny people against the vast, powerful, victorious empires
surrounding it. This ideology was the essential element which made it
possible for Israel to survive the dramatic onslaught against it. Yahweh
was transformed from the god of a semi-nomadic people into a cosmic,

universal God with a special relationship to Israel. Yahweh eventually to became their exclusive God.

This small, powerless people developed the grandest, most powerful deity, possibly because of their powerlessness. From Yahweh, they gained the strength required to survive. It was He who determined history and He controlled empires and emperors. Their new idea of God served in good and bad times.

The Deuteronomic authors and editors (of the books of Deuteronomy through II Kings) applied this principle to the history of their people: they succeeded when they obeyed Yahweh, and were punished for their disobedience. Yahweh was real and always prevailed.

A REPRISE ON HOW MONOTHEISM GREW

The major ideologues of this new view of God were Amos, Jeremiah, and Isaiah of the Exile.

- Amos made it clear that Yahweh was the God of all nations, not only of Israel and Judaea. Furthermore, he warned that Yahweh would punish them for social sins.

- 150 years later, Jeremiah expanded on this approach. He added that survival of Israel depended not on geographical location or Temple worship but on loyalty to Yahweh. Yahweh was omnipresent and could be worshipped and obeyed wherever the Israelites lived.

- Isaiah, after the Exile, made it clear just how great this God was. He also exalted the role of Israel with the concepts of chosen-ness and mission, giving them the highest motivation for their survival. The God to whom they were attached was the only God, and they alone had a covenant, a special relationship to Him. Through this process, Israel gained a concept of God which gave them the essential motivation to survive as a special, identifiable people.

Through this sacralization of the Jewish people, the secular goal of survival was achieved.

Chapter Thirty-Four
The author's thesis

CONCLUSIONS

The Bible, with its twenty-four books covering Israel's history and ideology, may be seen as the library of ancient Israel. Most of the books relate to history in some form, but they also include legal codes, love poetry, stories of origins and heroes, philosophy and theology. While it was canonized about 100 A.D., the Bible contains records of ancient oral traditions, some of which may date back to the time of Abraham, ca. 1800 B.C. These traditions, together with court and royal records, were combined with collections of the writings of the prophets and others. They were written, rewritten and edited over time, reflecting the orientation of its latest editors. Fortunately, much of the earlier material was preserved, so that contradictory ideas are often found in the same book.

My thesis will extract and emphasize its secular contents, those portions of the Bible in which there are no mystical or other-worldly concerns. Events, in these secular portions, take place through the interaction of humans.

The Bible's later authors and editors lived in a time when Israel was a nation no longer; to compensate, they developed an ideology in which the power of God took the place of the more conventional power of a secular state. They recognized historical reality and understood that Israel could not survive as it had in their era of national power. They needed a new raison d'être.

When Israel had a monarchy with a powerful army, the people's identity came primarily through their nation and their king. When the northern ten tribes were conquered, exiled, and lost their identity, the ideologues of Judaea realized that they had to find another vision to ensure their survival as an identifiable people. They developed a God-centered ideology to provide the raison d'etre for their continued existence.

Israel, in its formative period, was similar to the many mini-states of the Fertile Crescent. Originally, it had tribal leaders. Subsequently, for its confrontation with the Philistines, it developed a monarchy that was most effectively established by David. As with Israel's political-military facet, its religious facet developed like that of other communities. It took the form of a sacrificial cult led by professional priests. Local sanctuaries abounded, even after a central sanctuary was built in Jerusalem during the reign of Solomon.

As is made clear in the Bible, the Israelites paid homage to many deities through sacrifices in various sanctuaries. Gradually, Israel made the move from polytheism (recognizing many gods) to monolatry (placing their god above all others), then to monotheism (belief in a single, all-powerful, all-knowing God). It was this God who made a covenant with Israel, choosing them as his special people, a people with a holy mission. Thus Israel went from being a people like all others in the Middle East to a people unlike any other.

We need to scan the Bible to follow that staging: it's not presented in an orderly way. Gradually, Israelite society was presented as a holy society with a commitment to God going back to its founder, Abraham. The community was given sacred significance; its history was now viewed to be controlled by God. God used humans to carry out his will; their obedience or disobedience toward his commandments determined what would happen to them. The narratives about Israel were, to a great extent, taken out of the historical realm to be placed in a new 'historic' framework: one, in which the history of the people progressed under God's guidance.

Despite the efforts of its editors, there is an abundance of material that can be extracted from the Bible to shows the fundamentally secular nature of early Israelite society. That society sometimes picked up and moved, as when Nehemiah rebuilt the defenses of Jerusalem. He reordered its social structure with a passive God in the background. But prophets contemporary with Nehemiah continued to teach that God was still active, he'd protect Israel and punish its enemies. And these enemies would themselves come to recognize the one true God.

Human society survives when it deals with its problems in realistic, concrete terms. Flights of fancy into the supernatural realm may temporarily bring relief from harsh reality, but confrontation with the forces of history is the only path to success and survival. Encountering duress, ancient Israel turned to a powerful, protecting God as a motivating ideology. But this approach developed only when they no longer had an effective government and army to protect them.

The Bible presents both approaches. In the book of Exodus, God is a powerful liberator and war-leader who brought freedom to the children of Israel, and enabled them to enter and conquer Canaan, the Promised Land.

In the book of Esther it was humans, Esther and Mordecai, using their positions at court and their guile, who saved their fellow Israelites from death.

David achieved success in completely secular ways: gaining power gradually, even aligning himself with the Philistine enemy. Over time, he defeated the forces of Saul and united the disparate Israelite tribes. The presence of God is interspersed into the Davidic narratives, but when all such references are eliminated, his realm plays out as totally secular and historical.

The Bible, as we now have it, is a faith document. It was created to help Israel adapt to its status as a non-national or trans-national people for whom the Bible became their portable Promised Land, giving them purpose and hope. This allowed them alone, of all the peoples of the ancient Middle East, to survive as an identifiable group. They did it by adapting their religion to their socio-political situation.

However, there remains A BIBLE WITHIN THE BIBLE which reflects the secular nature of Israelite society from its beginnings through the last recorded period.

We call this THE SECRET BIBLE.

Chapter Thirty-Five

SELECTED BIBLIOGRAPHY

While it is clear to me that there is a secular Bible within the Bible, the reader is advised to keep a Bible at hand to validate (or not) my conclusions and interpretations. Suggestions for Bibles, reference books and scholarly treatments of each book of the Bible follow. Most libraries will have many others. Major public libraries, as well as those of universities and seminaries, will provide a wide spectrum and scholarly works and specialized journals on the Bible and related fields.

BIBLES
Cogan, Michael, editor. <u>The New Oxford Annotated Bible</u>. New York: Oxford University Press, 2001. (Translations of each book of the Bible with critical notes and introductory essays.)

Berlin, Adele and Brettler, Marc Zvi, editors. <u>The Jewish Study Bible</u>. New York: Oxford University Press, 2004. (The translation in this book is that published by the Jewish Publication Society in 1985. It includes excellent essays on biblical interpretation from antiquity until the present as well as other essays on the development of the Bible and other specialized subjects. Detailed notes on all aspects of the biblical text are included, primarily from Jewish sources).

REFERENCE BOOK
Mays, James L., editor. <u>The HarperCollins Bible Commentary</u>. New York: HarperCollins Publishers, 2000 (In addition to seven introductory essays, each book of the Bible is introduced with a detailed essay about the book and a commentary encompassing the entire text, with a brief bibliography of recent research on the particular book of the Bible.)

GENESIS
Sarna, N. M. <u>Understanding Genesis</u>. New York: Schocken: 1970.
Vawter, Bruce. <u>On Genesis: A New Reading</u>. Garden City, N. J.: Doubleday, 1977.

EXODUS
Childs, B.S. The Book of Exodus: A Critical Theological Commentary. Philadelphia: Westminster, 1974.
 Sarna, N.M. Exploring Exodus. New York: Schocken, 1986.
LEVITICUS
Budd, P. J. Leviticus. Grand Rapid, MI: Eerdmans, 1996.
Gorman, F.H. Jr. Leviticus: Divine Presence and Community. Grand Rapids, MI: Eerdmans, 1997.
NUMBERS
Milgrom, J. Numbers. Philadelphia: Jewish Publication Society, 1990.
Olson, D. T. Numbers. Louisville, KY: John Knox, 1996.

DEUTERONOMY
Mann, T. W. Deuteronomy. Louisville, KY: Westminster John Knox, 1995.
Tigay, J. H. Deuteronomy. Philadelphia: Jewish Publication Society, 1996.
JOSHUA
Boling, R.G. Joshua. Garden City, N. Y.: Doubleday, 1982.
Nelson, R. D. Joshua: A Commentary. Louisville, KY: Westminster John Knox, 1997.
JUDGES
Boling, R. G. Judges. Garden City, N. Y.: Doubleday, 1975.
Soggin, J. A. Judges. Translated by J. Bowden. Philadelphia: Westminster, 1981.
SAMUEL 1
McCarter, P. K. 1 Samuel. Garden City, N. Y.: Doubleday, 1980.
Polzin, Robert. Samuel and the Deuteronomist: 1 Samuel. San Francisco: Harper and Row, 1989.
SAMUEL 2
Brueggemann, W. First and Second Samuel. Louisville, KY: Westminster John Knox, 1990.
McCarter, P. K. II Samuel. Garden City, N. Y.: Doubleday, 1984.
KINGS 1 and 2
Nelson, R. D. First and Second Kings. Atlanta, GA: John Knox, 1987.
Provan, I. W. 1 and 2 Kings. Peabody, MA: Hendrickson, 1995.
CHRONICLES 1 and 2
Japhet, S. I and II Chronicles. Louisville, KY: Westminster John Knox, 1993.

Williamson, H. G. M. 1 and 2 Chronicles. Grand Rapids, MI: Eerdmans, 1982.

EZRA-NEHEMIAH

Blenkinsopp, J. Ezra-Nehemiah. Philadelphia: Westminster, 1988.

Clines, D. J. Ezra, Nehemiah, Esther. Grand Rapids, MI: Eerdmans, 1984.

ESTHER

Levenson, J. D. Esther: A Commentary. Louisville, KY: Westminster John Knox, 1997.

Moore, C. A. Esther. Garden City, NY: Doubleday, 1971,

JOB

Habel, N. C. The Book of Job: A Commentary. Philadelphia: Westminster, 1985.

Pope, M. H. Job: Introduction, Translation and Notes (3rd edition). Garden City, NY: Doubleday, 1973.

PSALMS

Anderson, B. W. Out of the Depths (Revised ed.). Louisville, KY: Westminster, 2000.

Brueggemann, W. The Message of the Psalms. Minneapolis, MN: Augsburg, 1984.

PROVERBS

Murphy, R. E. and Huweiler, E. Proverbs. Waco TX: Word Publishing, 1998.

Whybray, R. N. The Book of Proverbs. Cambridge: Cambridge University Press, 1972.

ECCLESIASTES

Longman, T. The Book of Ecclesiastes. Grand Rapids, MI: Eerdmans, 1997.

Seow, C. L. Ecclesiastes. New York: Doubleday, 1997.

SONG OF SONGS

Bloch, A. and C. The Song of Songs. New York: Random House, 1995.

Fox, M. V. The Song of Songs and the Egyptian Love Songs. Madison, WI: University of Wisconsin Press, 1985.

ISAIAH

Childs, B. The Book of Isaiah: A Critical, Theological Commentary. Louisville, KY: Westminster John Knox, 2000.

Blank, S. H. Prophetic Faith in Isaiah. New York: Harper and Brothers, 1958.

JEREMIAH

Brueggemann, W. Commentary on Jeremiah: Exile and Homecoming. Grand Rapids, MI: Eerdmans, 2996.

Clements, R. Jeremiah. Atlanta, GA: John Knox, 1988.

LAMENTATIONS

Provan, I. W. Lamentations. Grand Rapids, MI: Eerdmans, 1991.

Westermann, C. Lamentations. Issues and Interpretation. Minneapolis, MN: Fortress, 1994.

EZEKIEL

Blenknsopp, J. Ezekiel. Louisville, KY: John Knox, 1990.

Clements, R. E. Ezekiel. Louisville, KY: Westminster John Knox, 1996.

DANIEL

Hartman, L. F. and DiLella, A. The Book of Daniel. Garden City, NY: Doubleday, 1978.

Lacoque, A. The Book of Daniel. Translated by D. Pellauer. Atlanta, GA: Knox, 1979.

HOSEA

Anderen, F. I. and Freedman, D. N. Hosea: A New Translation with Introduction and Commentary. Garden City, NY: Doubleday, 1980.

Mays, J. L. Hosea. Philadelphia: Westminster, 1969.

JOEL

Birch, B. C. Hosea, Joel and Amos. Louisville, KY: Westminster John Knox, 1997.

Wolff, H. W. Joel and Amos. Philadelphia: Fortress, 1977.

AMOS

Auld, A. G. Amos. Sheffield: JSOT Press, 1986.

Mays, J. L. Amos. Philadelphia: Westminster, 1069.

OBADIAH

Raabe, P. R. Obadiah: A New Translation with Introduction and Commentary. New York: Doubleday, 1996.

Wolff, H. W. Obadiah and Jonah: A Commentary. Translated by M. Kohl. Minneapolis, MN: Augsburg, 1986.

JONAH

Limburg, J. Jonah: A Commentary. Louisville, KY: Westminster John Knox, 1993.

Sasson, J. Jonah. Garden City, NY: Doubleday, 2993.

MICAH

Hillers, D. Micah. Philadelphia, Fortress, 1984.

Mays, J. Micah. Philadelphia, Westminster, 1976.
NAHUM
Roberts, J. J. M. Nahum, Habakkuk, and Zephaniah. Louisville, KY: Westminster John Knox, 1991.
Spronk, K. Nahum. Kampen, Neetherlands: Kok Pharos, 1997.
HABAKKUK
Roberts: under Nahum
ZEPHANIAH
Berlin, A. Zephaniah: A New Translation with Introduction and Commentary. New York: Doubleday, 1994.
Roberts: under Nahum
ZECHARIAH
Meyers, C. and Meyers, E. Haggai, Zechariah 1-8 and Zechariah 9-14. New York: Doubleday, 1987 and 1993.
Redditt, P. Haggai, Zechariah and Malachi. Grand Rapids, MI: Eerdmans, 1995.
MALACHI
Hill, A. E. Malachi: A New Translation with Introduction and Commentary. New York: Doubleday, 1988.
Mason, R. The Books of Haggai, Zechariah and Malachi. Cambridge: Cambridge University Press, 1977.
HAGGAI
Redditt under Zechariah and Mason under Malachi